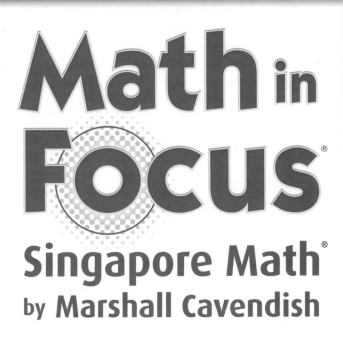
Math in Focus®
Singapore Math®
by Marshall Cavendish

Reteach

Author
Dr Fong Ho Kheong

Marshall Cavendish
Education

U.S. Distributor

Houghton
Mifflin
Harcourt

© 2015 Marshall Cavendish Education Pte Ltd

Published by Marshall Cavendish Education
An imprint of Marshall Cavendish Education Pte Ltd
Times Centre, 1 New Industrial Road, Singapore 536196
Customer Service Hotline: (65) 6213 9444
US Office Tel: (1-914) 332 8888 Fax: (1-914) 332 8882
E-mail: tmesales@mceducation.com
Website: www.mceducation.com

Distributed by
Houghton Mifflin Harcourt
222 Berkeley Street
Boston, MA 02116
Tel: 617-351-5000
Website: www.hmheducation.com/mathinfocus

First published 2015

Math in Focus® Reteach 4A
ISBN 978-0-544-19253-9

Printed in Singapore

2 3 4 5 6 7 8   1401   20 19 18 17 16 15
4500495934   A B C D E

Contents

Data and Probability

Fractions and Mixed Numbers

Introducing

Math in Focus®

Reteach

Reteach 4A and *4B*, written to complement *Math in Focus®: Singapore Math®* by *Marshall Cavendish* Grade 4, offer a second opportunity to practice skills and concepts at the entry level. Key vocabulary terms are explained in context, complemented by sample problems with clearly worked solutions.

Not all children are able to master a new concept or skill after the first practice. A second opportunity to practice at the same level before moving on can be key to long-term success.

Monitor students' levels of understanding during daily instruction and as they work on Practice exercises. Provide *Reteach* worksheets for extra support to students who would benefit from further practice at a basic level.

CHAPTER 1 Working with Whole Numbers

Worksheet 1   Numbers to 100,000

Write the missing numbers in the place-value chart.

Example

Ten Thousands	Thousands	Hundreds	Tens	Ones
●●●	●●●●●●●	●●●●	●●	●●●●●●●●●
3	7	4	2	8

1.

Ten Thousands	Thousands	Hundreds	Tens	Ones
●●●●●●●●●	●●●●●●	●●●●●●	●●●	

2.

Ten Thousands	Thousands	Hundreds	Tens	Ones
○○	○○○ ○○○ ○○	○○○ ○○○	○	○○ ○○

3.

Ten Thousands	Thousands	Hundreds	Tens	Ones
○○○ ○○○ ○		○○ ○○	○○○ ○○	○

4.

Ten Thousands	Thousands	Hundreds	Tens	Ones
○○○ ○○○	○○○ ○○○ ○○	○○○ ○○○ ○○○	○○○ ○○○ ○	○○○

Write each number in word form.

Example

32,572 _thirty-two thousand, five hundred seventy-two_____

5. 27,495 _____

6. 48,230 _____

7. 84,000 _____

8. 90,605 _____

Write each number in standard form.

Example

twelve thousand, seven hundred eleven   _12,711_

9.   fifty-two thousand, eight hundred   _____

10. eighty-three thousand, six hundred forty   _____

11. twenty-nine thousand, three hundred fifty-one _____

12. sixty thousand, two hundred eighty-four   _____

13. thirty-six thousand, five hundred sixteen   _____

14. seventy thousand, fourteen   _____

Complete the number patterns. Count on using ten thousands, thousands, hundreds, tens, or ones.

> *Example*
>
> 10,000   20,000   30,000   _40,000_   _50,000_   _60,000_

15.   50,000   60,000   70,000   _____   _____   _____

16.   19,000   19,010   19,020   _____   _____   _____

17.   30,400   30,500   30,600   _____   _____   _____

18.   40,500   50,600   60,700   _____   _____   _____

Write the missing numbers.

> *Example*
>
> 31,748 = ___3___ ten thousands + ___1___ thousand +
>
> ___7___ hundreds + ___4___ tens + ___8___ ones

19.   72,845 = _____ ten thousands + _____ thousands +

_____ hundreds + _____ tens + _____ ones

20.   24,319 = _____ ten thousands + _____ thousands +

_____ hundreds + _____ ten + _____ ones

21.   35,084 = _____ ten thousands + _____ thousands +

_____ hundreds + 84 ones

22.   91,600 = _____ ten thousands + _____ thousand +

_____ hundreds

● **Write the missing words.**

In 58,742,

> *Example*
>
> the digit 2 is in the _____*ones*_____ place.

23. the digit 4 is in the _____ place.

24. the digit 7 is in the _____ place.

25. the digit 8 is in the _____ place.

26. the digit 5 is in the _____ place.

● **Write the value of the digit 9 in each number.**

> *Example*
>
> 49,627 ____*9,000*____

27. 21,397 _____

28. 98,045 _____

29. 47,953 _____

30. 34,589 _____

Find each number using the clues.

> *Example*
>
> The digit 7 is in the thousands place.
> The digit 4 is in the ten thousands place.
> The digit 1 is in the tens place.
> The digit 2 is in the hundreds place.
> The digit 9 is in the ones place.
>
> The number is ___47,219___.

31.

The digit 8 is in the thousands place.
The digit 9 is in the ten thousands place.
The digit 5 is in the tens place.
The digit 6 is in the hundreds place.
The digit 3 is in the ones place.

The number is _____.

32.

The value of the digit 2 is 20.
The value of the digit 8 is 8,000.
The value of the digit 4 is 400.
The value of the digit 3 is 3.
The value of the digit 7 is 70,000.

The number is _____.

Name: _____   **Date:** _____

Write the missing numbers and words.

In 76,518,

> **Example**
>
> The value of the digit 5 is ___500___.

33. The digit 7 is in the _____ place.

34. The value of the digit 8 is _____.

35. The digit 6 is in the _____ place and its value is _____.

36. The value of the digit 1 is _____.

Complete the expanded form.

> **Example**
>
> 79,488 = ___70,000___ + ___9,000___ + ___400___ + ___80___ + ___8___

37. 42,859 = 40,000 + _____ + 800 + _____ + 9

38. 61,734 = _____ + 1,000 + _____ + 30 + _____

39. 24,570 = _____ + _____ + _____ + _____

40. 68,037 = _____ + _____ + _____ + _____ + _____

© Marshall Cavendish International (Singapore) Private Limited.

Name: _____ **Date:** _____

Complete the number patterns. Then write the rule for each pattern.

┌─ *Example* ───┐

20,427   30,427   40,427   _50,427_   _60,427_   70,427

Rule: _Add 10,000._

> Add 10,000 to 20,427 to get 30,427.
> Add 10,000 to 30,427 to get 40,427.
> So, the rule is to add 10,000 to find the next number in the pattern.

└───┘

41.   81,796   82,796   83,796   _____   _____   86,796

Rule: _____

42.   64,400   54,400   44,400   _____   _____   14,400

Rule: _____

43.   38,195   37,190   36,185   _____   _____   33,170

Rule: _____

Worksheet 2   Comparing Numbers to 100,000

Use the number line to count on or count back.
Write the missing numbers.

Example

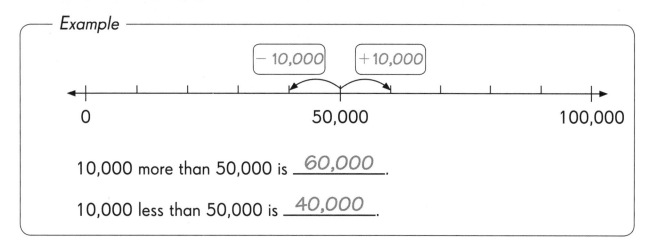

10,000 more than 50,000 is __*60,000*__.

10,000 less than 50,000 is __*40,000*__.

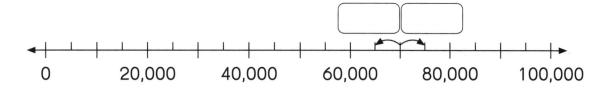

1.   5,000 more than 70,000 is _____.

2.   5,000 less than 70,000 is _____.

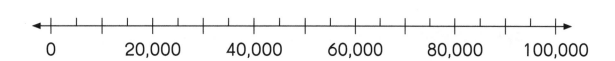

3.   10,000 more than 35,000 is _____.

4.   10,000 less than 45,000 is _____.

Compare the numbers in the place-value chart. Then write < or >.

Example

Ten Thousands	Thousands	Hundreds	Tens	Ones
9	5	0	0	2
9	2	1	7	4

95,002 92,174

> means *greater than*.
< means *less than*.

5.

Ten Thousands	Thousands	Hundreds	Tens	Ones
4	5	7	8	2
4	5	3	2	6

45,782 45,326

6.

Ten Thousands	Thousands	Hundreds	Tens	Ones
7	3	1	3	4
7	3	1	8	4

73,134 73,184

Look at the numbers in the place-value chart. Then order the numbers from least to greatest.

Example

Ten Thousands	Thousands	Hundreds	Tens	Ones
8	5	4	1	2
8	6	4	3	5
8	9	0	1	2

85,412   86,435   89,012   _____

Compare the value of each digit from left to right. The digits in the ten thousands place are the same. Next compare the digits in the thousands place.

7.

Ten Thousands	Thousands	Hundreds	Tens	Ones
3	7	4	8	2
5	2	1	0	4
5	8	3	6	9

_____

Write the missing numbers.

> **Example**
>
> 1,000 more than 97,136 is __98,136__.
>
> 31,072 is __50,000__ less than 81,072.

8.   10,000 more than 69,780 is _____.

9.   56,500 is _____ less than 60,500.

10.   1,000 less than 96,325 is _____.

11.   _____ is 30,000 more than 10,400.

Complete the number patterns. Then write the rule for each pattern.

> **Example**
>
> 43,200   45,200   47,200   __49,200__   __51,200__
>
> Rule: __Add 2,000.__

12.   67,700   62,700   57,700   _____   _____

Rule: _____

13.   52,378   55,478   _____   61,678   _____

Rule: _____

14.   _____   17,320   17,200   _____   16,960

Rule: _____

Name: _____ **Date:** _____

Worksheet 3 Adding and Subtracting Multi-Digit Numbers

Write the missing numbers.

1. Add the ones.

a. 4 ones + 8 ones = _____ ones

= _____ ten _____ ones
(note: 10 ones = 1 ten)

b. 7 ones + 6 ones = _____ ones

= _____ ten _____ ones

(7 + 6 = _____)

c. 5 ones + 9 ones = _____ ones

= _____ ten _____ ones

(5 + 9 = _____)

d. 8 ones + 7 ones = _____ ones

= _____ ten _____ ones

(8 + 7 = _____)

2. Add the tens.

a. 6 tens + 5 tens = _____ tens

= _____ hundred _____ tens
(note: 10 tens = 1 hundred)

b. 7 tens + 9 tens = _____ tens

= _____ hundred _____ tens

(70 + 90 = _____)

c.   3 tens + 8 tens = _____ tens

= _____ hundred _____ tens

(30 + 80 = _____)

d.   8 tens + 4 tens = _____ tens

= _____ hundred _____ tens

(80 + 40 = _____)

3.   Add the hundreds.

a.   3 hundreds + 9 hundreds = _____ hundreds

= _____ thousand _____ hundreds

(note: 10 hundreds = 1 thousand)

b.   6 hundreds + 8 hundreds = _____ hundreds

= _____ thousand _____ hundreds

(600 + 800 = _____)

c.   7 hundreds + 4 hundreds = _____ hundreds

= _____ thousand _____ hundreds

(700 + 400 = _____)

d.   8 hundreds + 2 hundreds = _____ hundreds

= _____ thousand _____ hundreds

(800 + 200 = _____)

4. Add without regrouping.

a.
$$
\begin{array}{r}
1,756 \\
+\ 3,223 \\
\hline
\end{array}
$$

b.
$$
\begin{array}{r}
2,468 \\
+\ 6,331 \\
\hline
\end{array}
$$

c.
$$
\begin{array}{r}
5,643 \\
+\ 2,345 \\
\hline
\end{array}
$$

d.
$$
\begin{array}{r}
4,769 \\
+\ 5,120 \\
\hline
\end{array}
$$

5. Add with regrouping.

a.
$$
\begin{array}{r}
4,232 \\
+\ 3,458 \\
\hline
\end{array}
$$

b.
$$
\begin{array}{r}
3,548 \\
+\ 2,287 \\
\hline
\end{array}
$$

c.
$$
\begin{array}{r}
5,941 \\
+\ 2,586 \\
\hline
\end{array}
$$

d.
$$
\begin{array}{r}
3,567 \\
+\ 4,596 \\
\hline
\end{array}
$$

6. Subtract.

    a. 9 ones − 4 ones = _____ ones   9 − 4 = _____

    b. 8 ones − 3 ones = _____ ones   8 − 3 = _____

7. Subtract.

    a. 12 ones − 8 ones = _____ ones   12 − 8 = _____

    b. 15 ones − 7 ones = _____ ones   15 − 7 = _____

    c. 14 ones − 9 ones = _____ ones   14 − 9 = _____

    d. 13 ones − 6 ones = _____ ones   13 − 6 = _____

8. Subtract.

    a. 3 tens − 7 ones = _____ tens 10 ones − 7 ones

                     = _____ tens _____ ones

                                 30 − 7 = _____

    b. 5 tens − 8 ones = _____ tens 10 ones − _____ ones

                     = _____ tens _____ ones

                                   50 − 8 = _____

c. 4 hundreds − 6 tens = _____ hundreds 10 tens − _____ tens

= _____ hundreds _____ tens

400 − 60 = _____

d. 2 thousands − 5 hundreds = _____ thousand _____ hundreds

− _____ hundreds = _____ thousand _____ hundreds

2,000 − 500 = _____

e. 6 hundreds − 7 tens = _____ hundreds _____ tens − _____ tens

= _____ hundreds _____ tens

600 − 70 = _____

f. 7 thousands − 9 hundreds = _____ thousands _____ hundreds

− _____ hundreds = _____ thousands _____ hundred

7,000 − 900 = _____

9. Subtract.

a.   6, 8 4 5
        − 2, 3 1 4
        _____

b.   4, 6 7 8
        − 3, 4 5 6
        _____

c.   3,472
   − 2,695

d.   2,463
   − 1,678

e.   5,000
   − 1,475

f.   7,000
   − 5,687

g.   62,435
   − 35,769

h.   73,241
   − 37,586

i.   30,000
   − 14,685

j.   80,000
   − 63,792

CHAPTER 2 Estimation and Number Theory

Worksheet 1   Estimation

**Find each sum or difference. Then use rounding
to check that your answer is reasonable.
Round each number to the nearest 100.**

Example

475 + 382 = ?

475 + 382 = ___857___

857 is close to 900, so the
answer is reasonable.

Number	Rounded to the nearest 100
475	500
382	400
Add	900

The estimated sum is ___900___.

Is your answer reasonable? ___Yes___

---

1.   Find 534 + 208.

534 + 208 = _____

Number	Rounded to the nearest 100
534	
208	
Add	

The estimated sum is _____.

Is your answer reasonable? _____

2.   Find 836 − 487.

836 − 487 = _____

Number	Rounded to the nearest 100
836	
487	
Subtract	

The estimated difference is _____.

Is your answer reasonable? _____

**Find each sum or difference. Then use rounding
to check that your answer is reasonable.
Round each number to the nearest 1,000.**

Example

$1,398 + 4,687 = ?$

$1,398 + 4,687 =$ ___6,085___

6,085 is close to
6,000, so the answer
is reasonable.

Number	Rounded to the nearest 1,000
1,398	1,000
4,687	5,000
Add	6,000

Is your answer reasonable? ___Yes___

---

3. Find $4,772 + 2,409$.

$4,772 + 2,409 =$ _____

Number	Rounded to the nearest 1,000
4,772	
2,409	
Add	

Is your answer reasonable? _____

4. Find 14,842 − 9,221.

14,842 − 9,221 = _____

Number	Rounded to the nearest 1,000
14,842	
9,221	
Subtract	

Is your answer reasonable? _____

Estimate each sum or difference using front-end estimation.

Example

7,389 − 2,543 = ?

⑦,389 − ②,543

___7,000___ − ___2,000___ = ___5,000___

The leading digit of 7,389 is 7.

The leading digit of 2,543 is 2.

5. 3,351 + 1,469   **6.** 9,217 − 2,881

Find each sum or difference. Then use front-end estimation to check that your answer is reasonable.

___ Example ___

478 + 403 = ___881___

④78   +   ④03
↓   ↓

Estimated sum: ___400___ + ___400___ = ___800___

Explain: _881 is close to 800, so the answer is reasonable._

7.   798 − 465 = _____

⑦98   −   ④65
↓   ↓

Estimated difference: _____ − _____ = _____

Explain: _____

8.   2,326 + 3,639 = _____

②,326   +   ③,639
↓   ↓

Estimated sum: _____ + _____ = _____

Explain: _____

9.   5,389 − 2,658 = _____

⑤,389   −   ②,658
↓   ↓

Estimated difference: _____ − _____ = _____

Explain: _____

Name: _____ Date: _____

Find each product. Then use rounding to check that your answer is reasonable.

Example

114 × 3 = ___342___

342 is close to 300, so the answer is reasonable.

Number	Rounded to the nearest 100 × 3
114	100 × 3 = 300

Is the answer reasonable? ___Yes___

10. 326 × 3 = _____

Number	Rounded to the nearest 100 × 3

Is the answer reasonable? _____

11. 267 × 2 = _____

Number	Rounded to the nearest 100 × 2

Is the answer reasonable? _____

**Find each product. Then use front-end estimation
to check that your answer is reasonable.**

> *Example*
>
> 79 × 5 = ____395____
>
> ⑦9   × 5
>   ↓
> ____70____ × 5 = ____350____
>
> The estimated product is ____350____.
>
> Explain: __395 is close to 350, so the answer is reasonable.__

12.   54 × 4 = _____

⑤4   × 4
   ↓

Estimated product: _____ × 4 = _____

Explain: _____

13.   112 × 3 = _____

①12   × 3
   ↓

Estimated product: _____ × 3 = _____

Explain: _____

Find each quotient. Then use related multiplication facts to check that your answer is reasonable.

Example

741 ÷ 3

741 ÷ 3 = ___247___

3 × 240 = 720

3 × 250 = 750

Estimated quotient:

750 ÷ 3 = ___250___

The answer is ___reasonable___.

```
      2 4 7
  3)7 4 1
    6 0 0
    1 4 1
    1 2 0
      2 1
      2 1
        0
```

Multiplication is the opposite of division.

741 is closer to 750 than 720. So, 741 ÷ 3 rounds to 750 ÷ 3.

---

14. 496 ÷ 4 = _____

4 × _____ = _____

4 × _____ = _____

Estimated quotient: _____ ÷ 4 = _____

The answer is _____.

15. 516 ÷ 2 = _____

_____ × _____ = _____

_____ × _____ = _____

Estimated quotient: _____ ÷ _____ = _____

The answer is _____.

16. $780 \div 5 = $ _____

_____ $\times$ _____ = _____

_____ $\times$ _____ = _____

Estimated quotient: _____ $\div$ _____ = _____

The answer is _____.

Solve. Decide whether to find an estimate or an exact answer.

> **— Example —**
>
> 724 meters of barbed wire is needed to enclose a park.
> How much barbed wire is needed to enclose 4 identical parks?
>
> 724 m $\times$ 4 = 2,896 m
>
> 2,896 meters of barbed
> wire is needed.
>
> > An exact answer is needed
> > because the question asks
> > **how much** barbed wire is
> > needed.

17.   Ms. Katy has $111. She wants to spend $52 on books, $33 on fruit, and
$21 on vegetables. Does she have enough money to buy all these things?

18. A bottle contains 784 milliliters of milk. A family drinks 309 milliliters of milk in the morning and the rest of the milk in the afternoon. How much milk do they drink in the afternoon?

19. Caithlin spent $14.99 on a sweater, $5.29 on 2 pairs of socks, and $8.99 on a blouse. About how much money did Caithlin spend in all?

Worksheet 2   Factors

Write the missing numbers.

> *Example*
>
> $14 \times 3 =$ ___42___
>
> ___42___ can be divided exactly by ___14___ and ___3___.

1. $21 \times 5 =$ _____

_____ can be divided exactly by 21 and _____.

2. $35 \times 3 =$ _____

_____ can be divided exactly by _____ and _____.

Write the missing numbers.

> *Example*
>
> $12 \times 3 =$ ___36___
>
> ___36___ is a product of 12 and 3.
>
> 12 and 3 are factors of ___36___.

Whole numbers can be broken into **factors**.

3. $8 \times 12 =$ _____

_____ is a product of 8 and 12.

_____ and _____ are factors of _____.

4. $26 \times 4 =$ _____

_____ is a product of 26 and 4.

_____ and _____ are factors of _____.

Find the quotient. Then write the missing words.

> *Example*
>
> $12 \div 4$
>
> $12 \div 4 = $ _____3_____
>
> Can 12 be divided exactly
>
> by 4? _____Yes_____
>
> Is 4 a factor of 12? _____Yes_____

When a number is divided exactly by another number, there is **no remainder**.

12 is divided exactly by 4. This means that 4 is a factor of 12.

5. $14 \div 5 = $ _____

Can 14 be divided exactly by 5? _____

Is 5 a factor of 14? _____

6. $18 \div 6 = $ _____

Can 18 be divided exactly by 6? _____

Is 6 a factor of 18? _____

7. $28 \div 7 = $ _____

Can 28 be divided exactly by 7? _____

Is 7 a factor of 28? _____

Find the factors of each number.

┌─ *Example* ───┐

8 = 1 × 8
   = 2 × 4

The factors of 8 are 1, 2, 4, and 8.

A whole number can be written as a product of factors.

└───┘

8.   24 = 1 × 24

        = 2 × _____

        = _____ × _____

        = _____ × 6

The factors of 24 are _____, _____, _____, _____, _____,

_____, _____, and _____.

9.   54 = _____ × _____

        = _____ × _____

        = _____ × _____

        = _____ × _____

The factors of 54 are _____, _____, _____, _____, _____,

_____, _____, and _____.

10. $72 =$ _____ $\times$ _____

      $=$ _____ $\times$ _____

      $=$ _____ $\times$ _____

      $=$ _____ $\times$ _____

      $=$ _____ $\times$ _____

      $=$ _____ $\times$ _____

The factors of 72 are _____, _____, _____, _____, _____,

_____, _____, _____, _____, _____, _____, and _____.

11. $108 =$ _____ $\times$ _____

      $=$ _____ $\times$ _____

      $=$ _____ $\times$ _____

      $=$ _____ $\times$ _____

      $=$ _____ $\times$ _____

      $=$ _____ $\times$ _____

The factors of 108 are _____, _____, _____, _____, _____,

_____, _____, _____, _____, _____, _____, and _____.

Divide. Then answer each question.

___ Example ___

15 ÷ 2 = ___7 R 1___

16 ÷ 2 = ___8___

A common factor is a factor that is shared by two or more numbers.

Is 2 a common factor of 15 and 16? ___No___

12.   48 ÷ 3 = _____

52 ÷ 3 = _____

Is 3 a common factor of 48 and 52? _____

13.   70 ÷ 5 = _____

95 ÷ 5 = _____

Is 5 a common factor of 70 and 95? _____

14.   45 ÷ 8 = _____

96 ÷ 8 = _____

Is 8 a common factor of 45 and 96? _____

Find the factors of each pair of numbers. Then circle the common factors.

Example

12 and 21

12: ①, 2, ③, 4, 6, 12

21: ①, ③, 7, 21

Which of the circled common factors is the greatest? _____3_____

15.   21 and 28

21: _____

28: _____

Which of the circled common factors is greatest? _____

16.   32 and 42

32: _____

42: _____

Which of the circled common factors is the greatest?

17.   48 and 72

48: _____

42: _____

Which of the circled common factors is the greatest? _____

Find the greatest common factor of each pair of numbers.

--- Example ---

16 and 24

Step 1   Divide 16 and 24 by a common factor.

$$2 \ | \ \overline{16, 24}$$
$$ 8, 12$$

16 ÷ 2 = 8, 24 ÷ 2 = 12

Step 2   Divide until 16 and 24 cannot be divided by a common factor other than 1.

$$2 \ | \ \overline{16, 24}$$
$$2 \ | \ \overline{8, 12}$$
$$2 \ | \ \overline{4, 6}$$
$$ 2, 3$$

2 and 3 have no common factor other than 1.

Step 3   Multiply the common factors.

2 × 2 × 2 = 8

The greatest common factor is 8.

18.   12 and 24

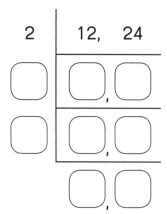

___ × ___ × ___ = ___

The greatest common factor is ____.

19.   36 and 42

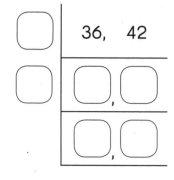

___ × ___ = ___

The greatest common factor is ____.

20.   54 and 72

21.   15 and 42

Answer the questions using these numbers.

10   15   24   36   54   75

Example

Which of the numbers have 2 as a factor?

10, 24, 36, and 54

22. Which of the numbers have 3 as a factor?

_____

23. Which of the numbers have 5 as a factor?

_____

24. Which of the numbers have 3 and 5 as factors?

_____

Find the factors of each number. Then decide whether the number is a prime number.

Example

$17 = 1 \times 17$

The factors of 17 are 1 and 17.
So, 17 is a prime number.

A **prime number** has only 2 different factors, 1 and itself.

25. 5

26. 9

27. 11

28. 26

Name: _____   Date: _____

**Find the factors of each number. Then decide whether
the number is a composite number.**

Example

$6 = 1 \times 6$
$ = 2 \times 3$

The factors of 6 are 1, 2, 3, and 6.
So, 6 is a composite number.

> A **composite number** has
> more than 2 different factors.

---

29.   20   **30.**   13

31.   63   **32.**   41

Which numbers in Exercises 29 to 32 are prime numbers?

33.   The prime numbers are _____ and _____.

34.   Why did you choose those two numbers? Explain your reasoning.

_____

_____

Worksheet 3   Multiples

Find the first eight multiples of each number.

A multiple of a number is the number multiplied by any whole number.

Example

$1 \times 4 = 4$	$2 \times 4 = 8$	$3 \times 4 = 12$	$4 \times 4 = 16$
$5 \times 4 = 20$	$6 \times 4 = 24$	$7 \times 4 = 28$	$8 \times 4 = 32$

The first eight multiples of 4 are ___4___, ___8___, ___12___,

___16___, ___20___, ___24___, ___28___, and ___32___.

1.   6

$1 \times 6 = \boxed{}$ $2 \times 6 = \boxed{}$ $3 \times 6 = \boxed{}$ $4 \times 6 = \boxed{}$

$5 \times 6 = \boxed{}$ $6 \times 6 = \boxed{}$ $7 \times 6 = \boxed{}$ $8 \times 6 = \boxed{}$

The first eight multiples of 6 are _____.

2.   8

$1 \times 8 = \boxed{}$ $2 \times 8 = \boxed{}$ $3 \times 8 = \boxed{}$ $4 \times 8 = \boxed{}$

$5 \times 8 = \boxed{}$ $6 \times 8 = \boxed{}$ $7 \times 8 = \boxed{}$ $8 \times 8 = \boxed{}$

The first eight multiples of 8 are _____.

Circle the numbers that are not multiples of the given number.

> **Example**
>
> 4: 4, (14), 16, 20, (34), 44
>
>
>
> 4 is a factor of all the multiples of 4.
> The numbers 4, 16, 20, and 44 can be divided exactly by 4. So, they are multiples of 4.

3.   3: 12, 15, 18, 21, 23

4.   5: 5, 15, 25, 51, 55

5.   7: 7, 17, 21, 27, 35, 42, 56, 63

6.   9: 18, 36, 39, 45, 47, 49, 54, 63, 72, 79

Check (✔) the correct box. Then write the missing numbers and words.

> **Example**
>
> Is 14 a multiple of 2?
>
> ```
>       7
>   2) 1 4
>      1 4
>     ─────
>        0
> ```
>
>
>
> Use division to determine whether a number is a multiple of another number.
>
> [✔] Yes, 14 is the ____seventh____ multiple of 2.
>
> [ ] No, 14 is not a multiple of 2. It cannot be divided exactly by 2.

7. Is 24 a multiple of 3?

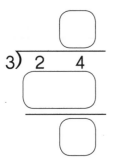

⬚ Yes, 24 is the _____ multiple of 3.

⬚ No, 24 is not a multiple of 3. It cannot be divided exactly by 3.

8. Is 45 a multiple of 6?

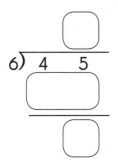

⬚ Yes, 45 is the _____ multiple of 6.

⬚ No, 45 is not a multiple of 6. It cannot be divided exactly by 6.

9. Is 96 a multiple of 8?

⬚ Yes, 96 is the _____ multiple of 8.

⬚ No, 96 is not a multiple of 8. It cannot be divided exactly by 8.

Name: _____   **Date:** _____

Circle the common multiples of each pair of numbers. Then write the missing numbers.

Example

3:    3, 6, 9, (12), 15, 18, 21, (24), 27

4:    4, 8, (12), 16, 20, (24), 28, 32, 36

> A **common multiple** is a multiple that is shared between two or more numbers.

The common multiples are ____12____ and ____24____.

> The **least common multiple** is the common multiple that is less than all the others.

The least common multiple is ____12____.

---

10.   5:   5, 10, 15, 20, 25, 30, 35, 40, 45

7:    7, 14, 21, 28, 35, 42, 49, 56, 63

The common multiple is _____.

The least common multiple is _____.

11.   6:   6, 12, 18, 24, 30, 36, 42, 48, 54

8:    8, 16, 24, 32, 40, 48, 56, 64, 72

The common multiples are _____ and _____.

The least common multiple is _____.

Find the first two common multiples of each pair of numbers.
Circle them and then write the least common multiple.

> *Example*
>
> 3 and 7
>
> 3:   3, 6, 9, 12, 15, 18, (21), 24, 27, 30, 33, 36, 39, (42)
>
> 7:   7, 14, (21), 28, 35, (42), 49
>
> The least common multiple is ____21____.

12.   2 and 5

   2: _____

   5: _____

   The least common multiple is _____.

13.   6 and 9

   6: _____

   9: _____

   The least common multiple is _____.

Find the least common multiple of each pair of numbers using division.

Example

8 and 16

| Step 1 | Divide 8 and 16 until they cannot be divided by a common factor other than 1. |

There are five factors.

2	8, 16
2	4, 8
2	2, 4
	1, 2

1 and 2 have no common factor other than 1.

| Step 2 | Multiply the factors. |

$2 \times 2 \times 2 \times 1 \times 2 = 16$

16 is the least common multiple of 8 and 16.

---

14. 9 and 18

15. 14 and 28

16. 15 and 45

17. 12 and 52

Worksheet 4   Multiplying Using Models

1.   Study the array. Write a multiplication statement from the given diagram.

a.

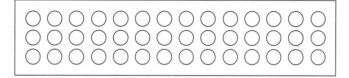

_____

b.

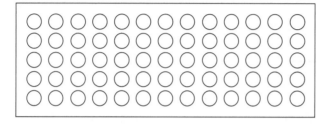

_____

c.

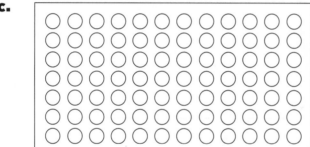

_____

2.   Color dots to show the multiplication statement. Use white dots as 1 one.
Cross out those unused dots.

a.   2 × 15

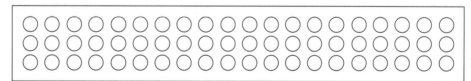

b.   4 × 19

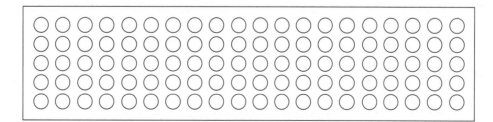

3. Study the diagram. Then write a multiplication statement.

a.

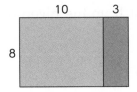

8 × _____ = _____ × _____ + _____ × _____

= _____ + _____

= _____

b.

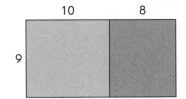

9 × _____ = ____ × _____ + ____ × _____

= ____ + ____

= _____

4. Complete to show the multiplication.

a. 7 × 14 → 7 × _____ = _____ , 7 × _____ = _____

So, 7 × 14 = _____ + _____ = _____

b. 5 × 18 → _____ × 10 = _____ , _____ × 8 = _____

So, 5 × 18 = _____ + _____ = _____

c. 2 × 16 → 2 × _____ = _____ , _____ × 6 = _____

So, 2 × 16 = _____ + _____ = _____

d. 6 × 15 → _____ × 10 = _____ , 6 × _____ = _____

So, 6 × 15 = _____ + _____ = _____

5.   Complete to show the multiplication.

  a. $6 \times 13 =$ _____ $\times$ _____ $+$ _____ $\times$ _____

  $=$ _____ $+$ _____

  $=$ _____

  b. $4 \times 23 =$ _____ $\times$ _____ $+$ _____ $\times$ _____

  $=$ _____ $+$ _____

  $=$ _____

  c. $5 \times 37 =$ _____ $\times$ _____ $+$ _____ $\times$ _____

  $=$ _____ $+$ _____

  $=$ _____

6.   Multiply

  a. $\begin{array}{r} 1\,8 \\ \times7 \\ \hline \end{array}$

  b. $\begin{array}{r} 2\,4 \\ \times9 \\ \hline \end{array}$

  c. $\begin{array}{r} 3\,5 \\ \times6 \\ \hline \end{array}$

  d. $\begin{array}{r} 4\,7 \\ \times5 \\ \hline \end{array}$

  e. $\begin{array}{r} 2\,9 \\ \times8 \\ \hline \end{array}$

CHAPTER 3 Whole Number Multiplication and Division

Worksheet 1 Multiplying by a 1-Digit Number

Complete the multiplication by ones. Then regroup into tens and ones if possible.

> **Example**
>
> 3 ones × 3 = _____9_____ ones

1.   4 ones × 2 = _____ ones

2.   7 ones × 4 = 28 ones

= _____ tens _____ ones

3.   8 ones × 6 = _____ ones

= _____ tens _____ ones

Complete the multiplication by tens. Then regroup into hundreds and tens.

> **Example**
>
> 7 tens × 4 = _____28_____ tens
>
> = _____2_____ hundreds _____8_____ tens

4.   4 tens × 5 = _____ tens

= _____ hundreds

5.   6 tens × 7 = _____ tens

= _____ hundreds _____ tens

Complete the multiplication by hundreds. Then regroup into thousands and hundreds.

Example

2 hundreds × 9 = 18 hundreds

= ___1___ thousand ___8___ hundreds

---

6. 3 hundreds × 6 = _____ hundreds

= _____ thousand _____ hundreds

7. 7 hundreds × 4 = _____ hundreds

= _____ thousands _____ hundreds

8. 8 hundreds × 6 = _____ hundreds

= _____ thousands _____ hundreds

9. 5 hundreds × 8 = _____ hundreds

= _____ thousands

Multiply and find the missing numbers.

Example

3,821 × 4 = ?

	3,	8	2	1
×				4

(superscript: 3)

(1)(5),(2)(8)(4)

Step 1

Multiply 1 one by 4.

1 one × 4 = _____4_____ ones

Step 2

Multiply 2 tens by 4.

2 tens × 4 = _____8_____ tens

Step 3

Multiply 8 hundreds by 4.

8 hundreds × 4 = _____32_____ hundreds

= _____3_____ thousands _____2_____ hundreds

Step 4

Multiply 3 thousands by 4.

3 thousands × 4 = _____12_____ thousands

Add the thousands.

_____12_____ thousands + 3 thousands = _____15_____ thousands

So, 3,821 × 4 = _____15,284_____.

10.   5,632 × 3

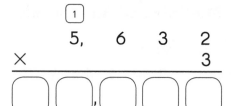

> **Step 1**
> 2 ones × 3 = _____ ones

> **Step 2**
> 3 tens × 3 = _____ tens

> **Step 3**
> 6 hundreds × 3 = _____ hundreds
>
>   = 1 thousand _____ hundreds

> **Step 4**
> 5 thousands × 3 = 15 thousands

Add the thousands.

15 thousands + 1 thousand = _____ thousands

So, 5,632 × 3 = _____.

11. $5,819 \times 5$

$$
\begin{array}{r}
\boxed{} \quad\;\; \boxed{4} \\
5,\;\; 8 \;\; 1 \;\; 9 \\
\times \qquad\qquad\quad 5 \\
\hline
\boxed{2}\,\boxed{9},\boxed{}\,\boxed{}\,\boxed{}
\end{array}
$$

Step 1
9 ones $\times$ 5 = 45 ones

= 4 tens _____ ones

Step 2
1 ten $\times$ 5 = _____ tens

Add the tens.

_____ tens + 4 tens = _____ tens

Step 3
8 hundreds $\times$ 5 = 40 hundreds

= _____ thousands

Step 4
5 thousands $\times$ 5 = _____ thousands

Add the thousands.

_____ thousands + _____ thousands = 29 thousands

So, $5,819 \times 5 =$ _____.

12.   8,720 × 4

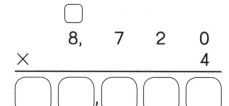

Step 1
0 ones × 4 = _____ ones

Step 2
2 tens × 4 = _____ tens

Step 3
7 hundreds × 4 = _____ hundreds

= _____ thousands _____ hundreds

Step 4
8 thousands × 4 = _____ thousands

Add the thousands.

_____ thousands + _____ thousands = _____ thousands

So, 8,720 × 4 = _____.

© Marshall Cavendish International (Singapore) Private Limited.

13.   6,509 × 6

$$
\begin{array}{r}
\square \qquad \square \\
6,\ \ 5\ \ 0\ \ 9 \\
\times \qquad\qquad 6 \\
\hline
\bigcirc\bigcirc,\bigcirc\bigcirc\bigcirc
\end{array}
$$

Step 1

9 ones × 6 = _____ ones

= _____ tens _____ ones

Step 2

0 tens × 6 = _____ tens

Add the tens.

_____ tens + _____ tens = _____ tens

Step 3

5 hundreds × 6 = _____ hundreds

= _____ thousands

Step 4

6 thousands × 6 = _____ thousands

Add the thousands.

_____ thousands + _____ thousands = _____ thousands

So, 6,509 × 6 = _____.

14.　　4,768 × 7

$$\begin{array}{r} \square \quad \boxed{4} \quad \square \\ 4, \quad 7 \quad 6 \quad 8 \\ \times \qquad\qquad 7 \\ \hline \bigcirc \bigcirc , \bigcirc \bigcirc \bigcirc \end{array}$$

Step 1

8 ones × 7 = _____ ones

= _____ tens _____ ones

Step 2

6 tens × 7 = _____ tens

Add the tens.

_____ tens + _____ tens

= _____ tens

= _____ hundreds _____ tens

Step 3

7 hundreds × 7 = _____ hundreds

Add the hundreds.

_____ hundreds + 4 hundreds

= _____ hundreds

= _____ thousands _____ hundreds

Step 4

4 thousands × 7 = _____ thousands

Add the thousands.

_____ thousands + _____ thousands = _____ thousands

So, 4,768 × 7 = _____ .

Multiply.

15. 7,643 × 2

```
        □
      7, 6  4  3
  ×            2
  ─────────────────
  ◯◯,◯◯◯
```

16. 6,923 × 8

```
      □  □  □
      6, 9  2  3
  ×            8
  ─────────────────
  ◯◯,◯◯◯
```

Multiply using the place value of each digit.

Example

```
        8, 1 5 3
  ×           4
  ─────────────────
          1 2  →  3 × 4 = ___12___
        2 0 0  →  50 × 4 = ___200___
        4 0 0  →  100 × 4 = ___400___
    3 2, 0 0 0  →  8,000 × 4 = ___32,000___
  ─────────────────
    3 2, 6 1 2
```

17.

```
        5, 3  4  7
  ×              3
  ─────────────────
          ◯◯      →  7 × 3 = _____
        ◯◯◯      →  40 × 3 = _____
      ◯◯◯        →  300 × 3 = _____
  ◯◯,◯◯◯        →  5,000 × 3 = _____
  ─────────────────
  ◯◯,◯◯◯
```

18.

$$
\begin{array}{r}
4,\ 8\ \ 3\ \ 5 \\
\times \qquad\quad 7 \\
\hline
\end{array}
$$

⬭⬭ ⟶ 5 × 7 = _____

⬭⬭⬭ ⟶ 30 × 7 = _____

⬭,⬭⬭⬭ ⟶ 800 × 7 = _____

⬭⬭,⬭⬭⬭ ⟶ 4,000 × 7 = _____

⬭⬭,⬭⬭⬭

Multiply.

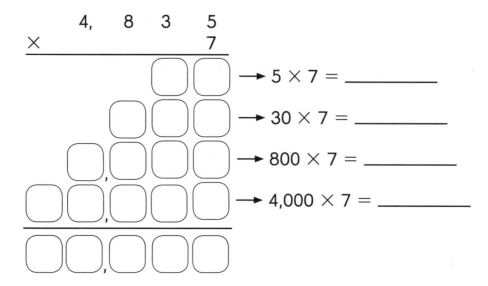

Example

$$
\begin{array}{r}
\boxed{2}\quad\boxed{2}\quad\ \\
2,\ \ 1\ \ 3\ \ 4 \\
\times \qquad\quad 7 \\
\hline
1\ \ 4,\ 9\ \ 3\ \ 8
\end{array}
$$

19.
$$
\begin{array}{r}
7\ \ 0\ \ 0 \\
\times \qquad 8 \\
\hline
\end{array}
$$
⬭,⬭⬭⬭

20.
$$
\begin{array}{r}
9\ \ 2\ \ 8 \\
\times \qquad 4 \\
\hline
\end{array}
$$
⬭,⬭⬭⬭

21.
$$
\begin{array}{r}
4,\ 7\ \ 2\ \ 6 \\
\times \qquad\quad 3 \\
\hline
\end{array}
$$
⬭⬭,⬭⬭⬭

22.
$$
\begin{array}{r}
9,\ 2\ \ 1\ \ 0 \\
\times \qquad\quad 6 \\
\hline
\end{array}
$$
⬭⬭,⬭⬭⬭

Worksheet 2 Multiplying by a 2-Digit Number

Write the missing numbers.

> *Example*
>
> 70 = ____7____ tens   9 tens = ____90____

1. 120 = _____ tens   **2.** 23 tens = _____

3. 800 = _____ hundreds   **4.** 6 hundreds = _____

5. 2,100 = _____ hundreds   **6.** 15 hundreds = _____

Multiply by tens.

> *Example*
>
> $4 \times 90 = ?$
>
> $4 \times 90 = 4 \times$ ___9___ tens
>
> $ = $ ___36___ tens
>
> $ = $ ___360___

7. $6 \times 80 = 6 \times$ _____ tens   **8.** $16 \times 30 = 16 \times$ _____ tens

$ = $ _____ tens $ = $ _____ tens

$ = $ _____ $ = $ _____

9. 21×5 tens = _____ tens = _____

10. 34×6 tens = _____ tens = _____

Multiply by hundreds.

> **Example**
>
> 6 × 4 hundreds = ____24____ hundreds = ____2,400____

11. 5 × 5 hundreds = _____ hundreds = _____

12. 11 × 300 = 11 × _____ hundreds

= _____ hundreds

= _____

Write the missing numbers.

> **Example**
>
> 75 × 20 = 75 × ____2____ × 10
>
> = ____150____ × 10
>
> = ____1,500____

13. 6 × 70 = 6 × _____ × _____

= _____ × 10

= _____

14. 74 × 90 = _____ × _____ × _____

= _____ × _____

= _____

Find each product.

> *Example*
>
> $12 \times 400 = ?$
>
> **Method 1**
>
> $12 \times 400 = 12 \times$ _____4_____ $\times 100$
>
> $\qquad\qquad = $ _____48_____ $\times 100$
>
> $\qquad\qquad = $ _4,800_
>
> **Method 2**
>
> $12 \times 400 = 12 \times$ _____100_____ $\times 4$
>
> $\qquad\qquad = $ _____1,200_____ $\times 4$
>
> $\qquad\qquad = $ _4,800_

15. $42 \times 200 = $ _____ $\times 100 \times$ _____

$\qquad\qquad = $ _____ $\times$ _____

$\qquad\qquad = $ _____

16. $973 \times 300 = $ _____ $\times 3 \times$ _____

$\qquad\qquad = $ _____ $\times$ _____

$\qquad\qquad = $ _____

Find each product.

--- Example ---

34 × 55 = ?

Step 1

Multiply 3 tens 4 ones by 5.
4 ones × 5 = 20 ones = 2 tens
3 tens × 5 = 15 tens
2 tens + 15 tens = 17 tens
Part of the product: 34 × 5 = 170

$$\begin{array}{r} \overset{2}{}\\ 3\ 4 \\ \times\ 5\ 5 \\ \hline 1\ 7\ 0 \end{array}$$

Step 2

Multiply 3 tens 4 ones by 50.
4 ones × 50 = 200 ones = 2 hundreds
3 tens × 50 = 150 tens = 15 hundreds
2 hundreds + 15 hundreds = 17 hundreds
Part of the product: 34 × 50 = 1,700

$$\begin{array}{r} \overset{2}{}\\ 3\ 4 \\ \times\ 5\ 5 \\ \hline 1\ 7\ 0 \\ 1,7\ 0\ 0 \end{array}$$

Step 3

Add the two parts of the product.
170 + 1,700 = 1,870

$$\begin{array}{r} \overset{2}{}\\ 3\ 4 \\ \times\ 5\ 5 \\ \hline 1\ 7\ 0 \\ 1,7\ 0\ 0 \\ \hline 1,8\ 7\ 0 \end{array}$$

17.

$$\begin{array}{r} 9\ \ 2 \\ \times\ \ 4\ \ 3 \end{array}$$

18.

$$\begin{array}{r} 3\ \ 6 \\ \times\ \ 5\ \ 7 \end{array}$$

┌─ *Example* ───┐

$172 \times 23 = ?$

          ²
     1 7 2
    $\times$ **2 3**
    5 1 6

Step 1

Multiply 172 by 3.
$172 \times 3 = 516$

   ¹
   ²
   1 7 2
 $\times$ **2** 3
  5 1 6
3,4 4 0

Step 2

Multiply 172 by 20.
$172 \times 20 = 3,440$

   ¹
   ²
  1 7 2
$\times$ 2 3
  5 1 6
3 4 4 0
3,9 5 6

Step 3

Add the two parts of the product.
$516 + 3,440 = 3,956$

So, $172 \times 23 =$ __3,956__.

└──┘

19.

```
      2  4  0
   ×     3  3
  ┌──┐┌──┐┌──┐
  └──┘└──┘└──┘
┌──┐┌──┐┌──┐┌──┐
└──┘└─,┘└──┘└──┘
  ┌──┐┌──┐┌──┐
  └─,┘└──┘└──┘
```

20.

```
      5  0  8
   ×     6  9
  ┌──┐┌──┐┌──┐┌──┐
  └──┘└──┘└──┘└──┘
┌──┐┌──┐┌──┐┌──┐
└──┘└─,┘└──┘└──┘
┌──┐┌──┐┌──┐┌──┐
└──┘└─,┘└──┘└──┘
```

21.

```
      9  0  0
   ×     8  1
   ┌──┐┌──┐┌──┐
   └──┘└──┘└──┘
┌──┐┌──┐┌──┐┌──┐
└──┘└──┘└─,┘└──┘
┌──┐┌──┐┌──┐┌──┐
└──┘└──┘└─,┘└──┘
```

22.

```
   6  3  7
   ×  7  5
  ┌──┐┌──┐┌──┐┌──┐
  └──┘└──┘└──┘└──┘
┌──┐┌──┐┌──┐┌──┐
└──┘└─,┘└──┘└──┘
┌──┐┌──┐┌──┐┌──┐
└──┘└─,┘└──┘└──┘
```

Use the number lines to round. Estimate each product.

Example

Estimate 47 × 36.

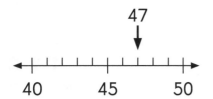

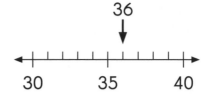

47 is closer to 50 than 40.   36 is closer to 40 than 30.

_____50_____ × _____40_____ = ____2,000____

47 × 36 is about ___2,000___.

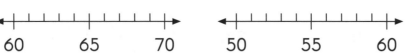

23. Estimate 68 × 52.

_____ × _____ = _____

68 × 52 is about _____.

24. Estimate 42 × 73.

_____ × _____ = _____

42 × 73 is about _____.

Use the number lines to round. Estimate each product.

Example

Estimate 44 × 560.

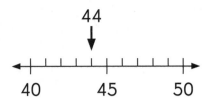

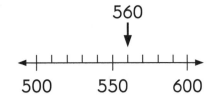

44 is closer to 40 than 50.   560 is closer to 600 than 500.

_____*40*_____ × _____*600*_____ = _____*24,000*_____

44 × 560 is about ___*24,000*___.

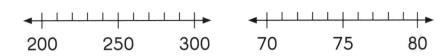

25.   Estimate 239 × 77.

_____ × _____ = _____

239 × 77 is about _____.

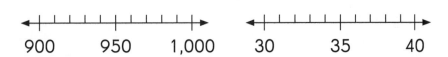

26.   Estimate 984 × 36.

_____ × _____ = _____

984 × 36 is about _____.

Name: _____   **Date:** _____

Multiply. Then estimate to check whether your answer is reasonable.

Example

$38 \times 94 = ?$

38 is closer to 40 than to 30.

94 is closer to 90 than to 100.

$$
\begin{array}{r}
{}^{7} \\
{}^{3} \\
3\ 8 \\
\times\ \ 9\ 4 \\
\hline
1\ 5\ 2 \\
3,\ 4\ 2\ 0 \\
\hline
3,\ 5\ 7\ 2 \\
\end{array}
$$

38×94 is about ____40____ × ____90____

= ____3,600____

3,572 is close to 3,600. So, the answer is reasonable.

---

27. $58 \times 27 =$ _____

Estimate: _____ × _____ = _____

Is the answer reasonable? Explain.

_____

_____

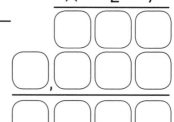

28. $63 \times 75 =$ _____

Estimate: _____ × _____ = _____

Is the answer reasonable? Explain.

_____

_____

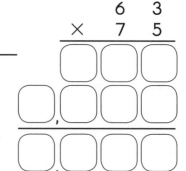

© Marshall Cavendish International (Singapore) Private Limited.

Multiply. Then estimate to check whether your answer is reasonable.

┌─ *Example* ──

26 × 246 = ?

> 26 is closer to 30 than to 20.
>
> 246 is closer to 200 than to 300.

$$
\begin{array}{r}
{}^{2}\;{}^{1}_{3}\;\;\; \\
2\;4\;6 \\
\times \quad 2\;6 \\
\hline
{}^{1}1,\,4\;7\;6 \\
4,\,9\;2\;0 \\
\hline
6,\,3\;9\;6
\end{array}
$$

26 × 246 is about ____30____ × ____200____

= ___6,000___

6,396 is close to 6,000. So, the answer is ___reasonable___.

└──

29. 137 × 34 = _____

Estimate: _____ × _____ = _____

The answer is _____.

30. 760 × 83 = _____

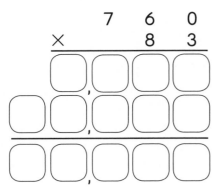

Estimate: _____ × _____ = _____

The answer is _____.

31.   822 × 97 = _____

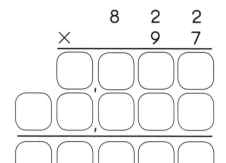

```
        8   2   2
    ×       9   7
    _____
   ( )( )( )( )
      ,
  ( )( )( )( )( )
      ,
  ( )( )( )( )( )
      ,
```

Estimate: _____ × _____ = _____

The answer is _____.

32.   485 × 79 = _____

```
        4   8   5
    ×       7   9
    _____
   ( )( )( )( )
      ,
  ( )( )( )( )( )
      ,
  ( )( )( )( )( )
      ,
```

Estimate: _____ × _____ = _____

The answer is _____.

Name: _____ Date: _____

Worksheet 3 Modeling Division with Regrouping

Complete the division steps.

--- Example ---

$468 \div 3 = ?$

$$\begin{array}{r} 1 \\ 3\overline{)4\ 6\ 8} \\ \underline{3\ 0\ 0} \\ 1 \end{array}$$

Step 1

Divide the hundreds by 3.
4 hundreds ÷ 3 = 1 hundred with 1 hundred left over

$$\begin{array}{r} 1 \\ 3\overline{)4\ 6\ 8} \\ \underline{3\ 0\ 0} \\ 1\ 6\ 8 \end{array}$$

Regroup the hundreds.
1 hundred = 10 tens

Add the tens.
10 tens + 6 tens = 16 tens

$$\begin{array}{r} 1\ 5 \\ 3\overline{)4\ 6\ 8} \\ \underline{3\ 0\ 0} \\ 1\ 6\ 8 \\ \underline{1\ 5\ 0} \\ 1\ 8 \end{array}$$

Step 2

Divide the tens by 3.
16 tens ÷ 3 = 5 tens with 1 ten left over

Regroup the tens.
1 ten = 10 ones

Add the ones.
10 ones + 8 ones = 18 ones

$$\begin{array}{r} 1\ 5\ 6 \\ 3\overline{)4\ 6\ 8} \\ \underline{3\ 0\ 0} \\ 1\ 6\ 8 \\ \underline{1\ 5\ 0} \\ 1\ 8 \\ \underline{1\ 8} \\ 0 \end{array}$$

Step 3

Divide the ones by 3.
18 ones ÷ 3 = 6 ones

So, $468 \div 3 =$ ___156___.

1.   580 ÷ 5

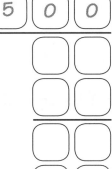

Step 1

5 hundreds ÷ 5 = _____1_____ hundred

Step 2

_____ tens ÷ 5

= _____ ten with _____ tens left over

Regroup the tens.

_____ tens = _____ ones

Step 3

_____ ones ÷ 5 = _____ ones

2.   968 ÷ 4

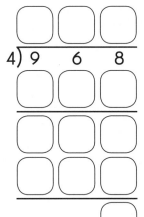

Step 1

9 hundreds ÷ 4

= _____ hundreds with _____ hundred left over

Regroup the hundred.

_____ hundred = _____ tens

Add the tens.

_____ tens + 6 tens = _____ tens

Step 2

_____ tens ÷ 4 = _____ tens

Step 3

8 ones ÷ 4 = _____ ones

© Marshall Cavendish International (Singapore) Private Limited.

3. $858 \div 6$

Step 1

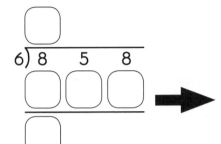

Step 2

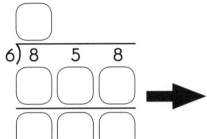

Step 3

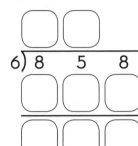

Step 5

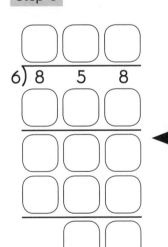

Step 4

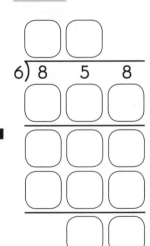

Name: _____ **Date:** _____

Divide. Write the missing numbers.

> *Example*
>
> $276 \div 3 = ?$
>
> ```
>        9   2
>   3) 2  7  6
>      2  7  0
>            6
>            6
>            0
> ```

4. $765 \div 9$

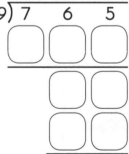

5. $472 \div 8$

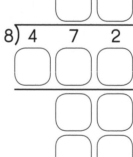

6. 903 ÷ 7

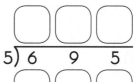
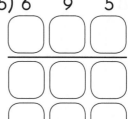

7. 695 ÷ 5

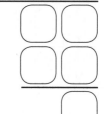

8. 578 ÷ 2

9. 867 ÷ 3

10.   984 ÷ 6

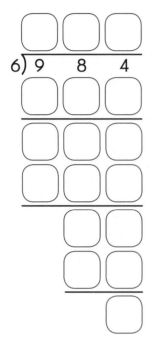

11.   672 ÷ 4

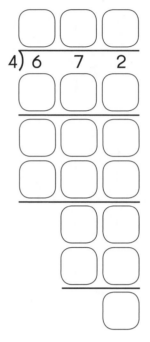

Worksheet 4   Dividing by a 1-Digit Number

Find each quotient.

Example

3,852 ÷ 3 = ?

Step 1

Divide 3 thousands by 3.
3 thousands ÷ 3 = 1 thousand
= 1,000

```
      1
 3) 3, 8 5 2
    3, 0 0 0
```

Step 2

Divide 8 hundreds by 3.
8 hundreds ÷ 3
= 2 hundreds with 2 hundreds left over
= 200 with 20 tens left over

```
      1, 2
 3) 3, 8 5 2
    3, 0 0 0
       8 5 2
       6 0 0
           2
```

Step 3

Divide 25 tens by 3.
25 tens ÷ 3
= 8 tens with 1 ten left over
= 80 with 10 ones left over

```
      1, 2 8
 3) 3, 8 5 2
    3, 0 0 0
       8 5 2
       6 0 0
       2 5 2
       2 4 0
           1
```

Step 4

Divide 12 ones by 3.
12 ones ÷ 3 = 4 ones

So, 3,852 ÷ 3 = ___1,284___.

```
      1, 2 8 4
 3) 3, 8 5 2
    3, 0 0 0
       8 5 2
       6 0 0
       2 5 2
       2 4 0
         1 2
         1 2
            0
```

A **quotient** is the answer to a division problem.

No remainder.

1.   4,692 ÷ 4

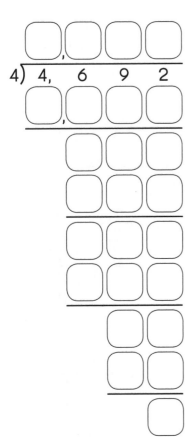

2.   7,326 ÷ 9

Find each quotient and remainder.

Example

$8,162 \div 6 = ?$

```
    1              1 3             1,3 6 0  ← quotient
6)8,1 6 2  →   6)8,1 6 2   →   6)8,1 6 2
  6,0 0 0        6,0 0 0         6,0 0 0
      2          2,1 6 2         2,1 6 2
                 1,8 0 0         1,8 0 0
                   3 6 2           3 6 2
                                   3 6 0
                                       2  ← remainder
```

$1,000 \times 6 = 6,000$

$300 \times 6 = 1,800$

$60 \times 6 = 300$

$8,162 \div 6 = \underline{1,360 \ R \ 2}$

3. $5,687 \div 9$

4. $9,395 \div 7$

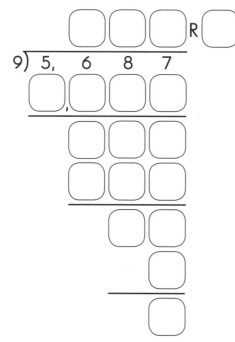

Estimate each quotient using related multiplication facts.

— *Example* —

184 ÷ 5 = ?

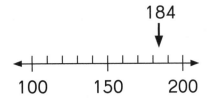

Related multiplication facts:

30 × 5 = 150   40 × 5 = 200

184 is closer to 200 than to 150.

So, 184 ÷ 5 is about 200 ÷ 5 = _____40_____.

5.   680 ÷ 6

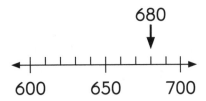

110 × 6 = _____   120 × 6 = _____

680 is closer to _____ than to _____.

So, 680 ÷ 6 is about _____ ÷ 6 = _____.

6. 6,882 ÷ 8

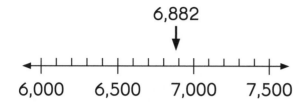

6,882

6,000   6,500   7,000   7,500

_____ × _____   _____ × _____

= _____   = _____

6,882 is closer to _____ than to _____.

So, 6,882 ÷ 8 is about _____ ÷ 8 = _____.

Divide. Then estimate to check whether your answer is reasonable.

Example

4,156 ÷ 6 = ?

```
      6 9 2 R 4      Estimate:
6)4,1 5 6
  3,6 0 0              4,200   ÷ 6 =   700
    5 5 6
    5 4 0           4,156 ÷ 6 is about   700   , so
      1 6
      1 2           the answer is   reasonable   .
        4
```

4,156 ÷ 6 =   692 R 4

7. 7,369 ÷ 5

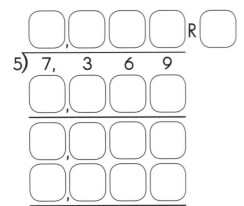

Estimate:

_____ ÷ 5 = _____

7,369 ÷ 5 is about _____, so

the answer is _____.

8. 6,750 ÷ 8

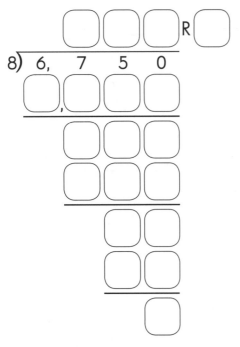

Estimate:

_____ ÷ 8 = _____

6,750 ÷ 8 is about _____, so

the answer is _____.

Worksheet 5   Real-World Problems: Multiplication and Division

Solve. Show your work.

Example

Mr. Jack pays $785 a month to rent an apartment.
Ms. Jill pays $1,075 a month to rent an apartment.
How much rent do they pay in 12 months?

| Step 1 | $785 + $1,075 = $1,860 |

| Step 2 | 12 × $1,860 = $22,320 |

They pay __$22,320__ in 12 months.

---

1.   Amos packs 298 boxes of pears each day.
Kim packs 509 boxes each day.
How many boxes of pears do they pack in 21 days?

Step 1

How many boxes of pears do they pack each day?

_____ + _____ = _____

Step 2

How many boxes of pears do they pack in 21 days?

_____ × 21 = _____

They pack _____ boxes of pears in 21 days.

Solve each problem using models.

Example

Mr. Collins saves $485 a month.
Mr. Hill saves twice as much as Mr. Collins.
How much do they save in 12 months?

Step 1   How much does Mr. Hill save?

$485

Mr. Collins

Mr. Hill

Mr. Hill saves $485 × 2 = _____$970_____ a month.

Step 2   How much do they save in a month?

$485 + _____$970_____ = _____$1,455_____

Step 3   How much do they save in 12 months?

$1,455 × 12 = _____$17,460_____

2.   Sam has 215 marbles. Tony has 4 times as many marbles as Sam.

Complete the model. Write the missing numbers.

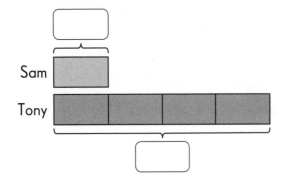

Sam

Tony

a. How many marbles does Tony have?

1 unit ⟶ _____

4 units ⟶ _____ × 4 = _____

Tony has _____ marbles.

b. Tony packs the marbles into boxes of 9 marbles each. How many full boxes does he have?

_____ ÷ 9 = _____ R _____

He has _____ full boxes.

c. How many marbles are not packed in a full box?

_____ marbles are not packed in a full box.

3. A school has 106 boys. There are 12 more girls than boys in the school.

Complete the model to show the number of girls.

106

Boys

Girls

a. How many students are there in the school?

There are _____ students in the school.

b. The school puts the children equally into 8 classes.
How many students are there in each class?

There are _____ students in each class.

4. Mr. Roberts has $782 to buy one computer and 2 mobile phones.
A computer costs twice as much as one mobile phone.
He needs $418 more to buy all the items.

Complete the model. Write the missing numbers.

| 1 computer |
| 2 mobile phones |

$\Big\}$ [ ] $+\$418$

a. What is the total cost of all the items?

The total cost of all the items is _____.

b. How much does the computer cost?

The computer costs _____.

5.   Ms. Leslie has $2,750 to spend on a table and 5 chairs.
The table costs 3 times as much as one chair. After buying all the items
she has $262 left.

Complete the model. Write the missing numbers.

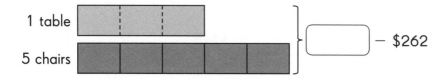

1 table

5 chairs

☐ – $262

a.   What is the total cost of all the items?

The total cost is _____.

b.   What is the cost of the 5 chairs?

The 5 chairs cost _____.

6. Sally sold twice as many boxes of chocolate cookies as Tina. Tina sold 78 boxes. Each box contains 12 packets of cookies.

a. How many packets of chocolate cookies did Tina sell?

There are _____ boxes of chocolate cookies.

There are _____ packets in each box.

_____ boxes × _____ packets = _____

Tina sold _____ packets of chocolate cookies.

b. How many packets of chocolate cookies does Sally have?

Sally sold twice as many packets as Tina.

So, 2 × _____ = _____

Sally sold _____ packets of chocolate cookies.

7. Jeff buys three times as many cartons of eggs as Andrew. Each carton has 12 eggs. Jeff has 25 cartons of eggs.

a. How many eggs does Jeff buy?

There are _____ cartons of eggs.

There are _____ eggs in each carton.

_____ cartons × _____ eggs = _____

Jeff buys _____ eggs.

b. How many eggs does Andrew buy?

Jeff buys 3 times as many as Andrew.

So, _____ ÷ _____ = _____

Andrew buys _____ eggs.

8. Sam packs twice as many boxes of presents as Lee. Each box contains 16 small packets of presents. Lee packs 69 boxes of presents altogether.

    a. How many packets of presents does Lee pack altogether?

    b. How many packets of presents does Sam pack altogether?

9. Klio packs her photos into boxes. She packs 5 times as many boxes as her brother Jack. Each box can contain 32 photos. Klio has 15 boxes in all.

    a. How many photos does Klio pack altogether?

    b. How many photos does Jack pack altogether?

CHAPTER 4 Tables and Line Graphs

Worksheet 1   Making and Interpreting a Table

Find the parts and wholes.

Example

The table shows the number of boys and girls in a school.

Number of Boys	Number of Girls	Total
625	648	**1,273**

part → 625

part → 648

You can find the whole by adding the parts.

You can find the parts by subtracting from the whole.

$625 + 648 = \underline{\quad 1,273 \quad}$

$1,273 - 625 = \underline{\quad 648 \quad}$ girls

---

1.   **Number of Vehicles in a Parking Lot**

Number of Cars	Number of Trucks	Total Number of Cars and Trucks
1,470		2,374

2.

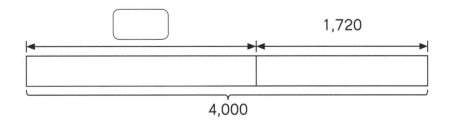

1,720

4,000

Complete.

┌─ *Example* ───┐

Luke wants to find out the type of transportion his school teachers use. Which questionnaire will give him the correct information?

a.

Transportation:
_____
Distance traveled:
_____

b.

Name:
_____
Transportation:
_____

c.

Transportation 1:
_____
Transportation 2:
_____

Questionnaire [*b*] will give him the correct information.

└───┘

3. Jessica wants to find out the types of pets her friends have owned. Which survey card will help her obtain the information she wants?

a.

Name: _____
Pet 1: _____
Pet 2: _____

b.

Pet: _____
Name 1: _____
Name 2: _____

Card [   ] will help her obtain the information.

Make tally marks to count the number of each type of pet.

These are the pets that Jessica's friends owned.

Example

Number of dogs   _____//// _____

---

4.   Number of cats   _____

5.   Number of hamsters   _____

6.   Number of fish   _____

7.   Number of other types of pets   _____

Complete the table using data from the tally marks.

8.

Type of Pet	Dog	Cat	Hamster	Fish	Other
Number	5				

A table can be used to organize and present data.

There are 5 tally marks for the number of dogs. So, there are 5 dogs.

Complete. Use the data in the tally chart.

The tally chart shows the number of animals kept on a farm.

Number of Animals

Animal	Number
cow	~~IIII~~ ~~IIII~~ ~~IIII~~ III
dog	III
chicken	~~IIII~~ ~~IIII~~ ~~IIII~~ ~~IIII~~ ~~IIII~~ ~~IIII~~ ~~IIII~~ I
duck	~~IIII~~ ~~IIII~~ II

> **Example**
>
> How many cows are there on the farm?
>
> _5 + 5 + 5 + 3 = 18_

9. There are _____ chickens.

10. There are twice as many chickens as there are _____.

11. How many fewer ducks are there than chickens? _____

12. There are _____ animals on the farm altogether.

Complete the table. Use the data on the cards.

Ms. Susan received some cards from her students stating their favorite sport.

Name: Arjun	Name: Chris	Name: Darwin
Favorite sport: Basketball	Favorite sport: Volleyball	Favorite sport: Volleyball

Name: Lee	Name: Claire	Name: Katy
Favorite sport: Cycling	Favorite sport: Basketball	Favorite sport: Basketball

Name: Megan	Name: Norris
Favorite sport: Soccer	Favorite sport: Cycling

13.

Sport	Tally	Number of Students
Basketball	///	3

Complete the table. Then answer the question.

The set of data shows the numbers that appeared each time a number cube was tossed.

1, 4, 6, 2, 5, 5, 6, 4, 5, 2, 1, 3, 3, 1, 4, 5, 2, 6, 1

14.

Number Shown	One					
Number of times tossed	4					

How many times was the number cube tossed? _____

Complete the table using the data from the tally chart.

The tally chart shows the number of people from different countries participating in a game.

Country	Number of Participants
USA	‖‖‖ ‖‖‖ ‖
France	‖‖‖ ‖‖‖ ‖‖‖ ‖‖‖
Kenya	‖‖‖ ‖‖‖ ‖‖‖
Singapore	‖‖‖ ‖‖‖
Russia	‖‖‖

15.

Country	USA					
Number of Participants	12					

What is the total number of participants? _____

© Marshall Cavendish International (Singapore) Private Limited.

Complete the table using the following words and numbers.
An example has been given in the table.

> Words: Tally; Number of Students; Favorite Fruit;
>   apple; orange; plum; apricot; pear
>
> Numbers: 5; 8; 2; 4; 7

Most students prefer apples.
The least number of students prefer plums.
More students prefer pears than oranges.
Fewer students prefer apricots than oranges.

16.

Favorite Fruit		Number of Students
apple	|||| |||	8

Complete. Use the data in the bar graph.

The bar graph shows the amount of rainfall recorded from January through June.

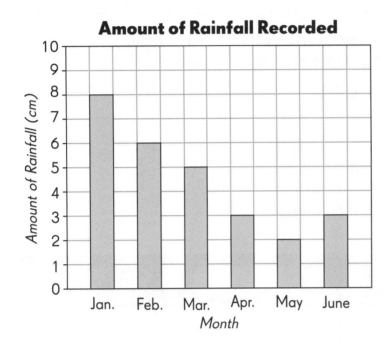

Amount of Rainfall Recorded

17.   Which month had the greatest amount of rainfall? _____

18.   Which month had the least amount of rainfall? _____

19.   What is the difference between the amount of rainfall in January and the amount of rainfall in March?

_____

20.   Which two months had the same amount of rainfall?

_____ and _____

21.   What is the total amount of rainfall from January through June?

_____

22.   Which month has three times the amount of rainfall as May?

_____

© Marshall Cavendish International (Singapore) Private Limited.

Draw a graph using the data in the table.

The table shows the number of students each school sent to compete in a mathematics quiz.

School	Number of Participants
School A	5
School B	9
School C	12
School D	18
School E	7

23.

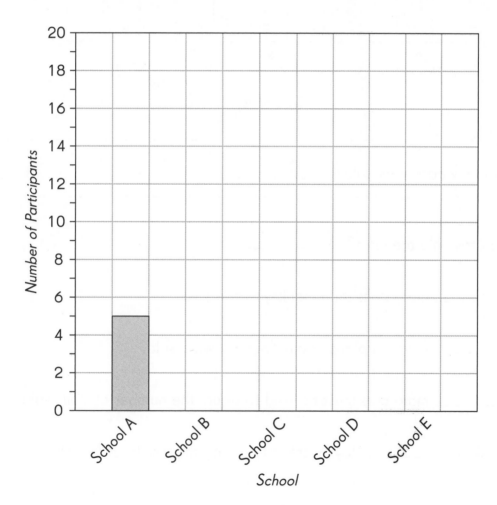

Complete. Use data from the bar graph.

The bar graph shows the number of toys sold in a shop during the month of March.

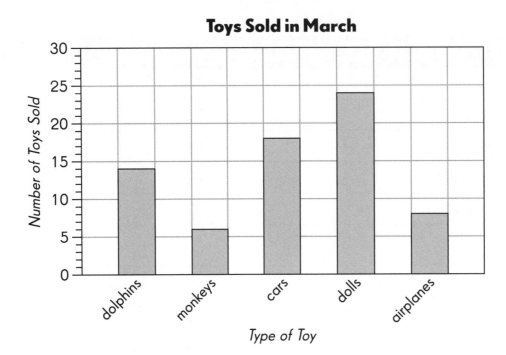

Toys Sold in March

┌─ *Example* ───┐
│   How many cars were sold? _____18_____   │
└──┘

24.   Which toy sold the most? _____

25.   _____ more dolls than monkeys were sold.

26.   _____ fewer airplanes than dolphins were sold.

27.   _____ more cars must be sold to equal the number of dolls sold.

28.   A total of _____ toys were sold during the month of March.

Worksheet 2   Using a Table

Find the data by studying the rows, columns, and intersections.

The table shows the departure times and destinations of some buses.

Bus Schedule

Step 1   Look under Destination for the row that shows Boston.

Destination	Departure 3 P.M.	Departure 5 P.M.	Departure 9 P.M.
Newark	X24	T48	U36
Cleveland	V11	S27	Y32
Boston	**W77**	P88	Q10

Step 2   Look across this row for a 3 P.M. departure.

Step 3   The intersection where the Boston row meets the 3 P.M. departure column shows W77.

— *Example* —

Mr. Sanchez wants to reach his home in Boston in time for dinner at 8 P.M. The bus journey takes about 4 hours. Which bus should he take to reach home in time for dinner?

4 hours after 3 P.M. is 7 P.M.

He should take bus __W77__.

1. Which buses go to Boston? _____, _____, and _____

2. Which buses depart at 5 P.M.? _____, _____, and _____

3.   The bus journey to Newark takes about 30 minutes. Which bus must

Mr. Daniels take to reach his home in Newark in the evening? _____

4.   Ms. Williams can only reach the bus station at 4.40 P.M. Which buses

can she take to Cleveland? _____ or _____

Complete. Use the data in the table.

The table shows the favorite fruit of a group of students.

Favorite Fruit of a Group of Students

Fruit	Number of Boys	Number of Girls	Total Number
Apple	20	22	42
Orange	8	7	15
Pear	9	14	23
Banana	21	13	34
Guava	4	6	10

Example

The greatest number of students prefer _____*apples*_____.

5.   The least number of students prefer _____.

6.   _____ more students prefer bananas to oranges.

7.   _____ more girls than boys prefer pears.

8.   32 fewer students prefer guavas to _____.

9.   There is a total of _____ boys in the survey.

Name: _____   Date: _____

Complete the table using the following data. Answer the questions.

- There are 200 students in a school.
- 76 students take the bus to school.
- 1 student takes a taxi to school.
- 54 students walk to school.
- 42 students cycle to school.
- Some students live on the school campus.

Example

How many students do not live on the school campus?

$76 + 1 + 54 + 42 = 173$

_____173_____ students do not live on the school campus.

10. How many students live on the school campus? _____

11. Complete the table.

Mode of Transportation	Bus	Taxi	Walk	Cycle
Number of Students				

12. Which is the least used mode of transportation? _____

13. How many students take the bus or cycle to school? _____

14. How many more students walk to school than cycle? _____

Complete the table.

The table shows the number of red and green apples sold on Monday through Friday.

Number of Apples Sold on Monday Through Friday

Day	Number of Green Apples	Number of Red Apples	Total Number of Apples
Monday	60	*80 − 60 = 20*	80
Tuesday	15	50	
Wednesday	30		100
Thursday		70	120
Friday	40		
Total			600

15. On which day was the greatest number of apples sold? _____

16. On which day was the least number of apples sold? _____

17. Which type of apples sold the most? _____

18. On which day was the number of green apples sold three times

the number of red apples sold? _____

19. How many more apples were sold on Friday than on Tuesday?

_____

Worksheet 3 Line Graphs

Complete. Use data from the line graph.

The line graph shows the price of mangoes.

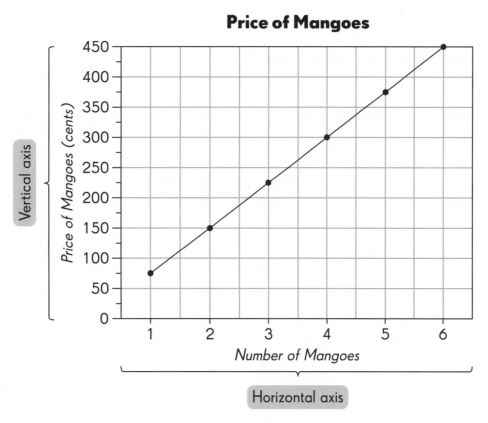

Price of Mangoes

Example

What is the cost of 1 mango?

Step 1	Find 1 along the horizontal axis.
Step 2	Move up until you meet a point on the graph.
Step 3	From that point on the graph, move left until you meet the vertical axis.
Step 4	The point on the vertical axis is 75 cents.

1 mango costs ___75 cents___.

1.   Find the cost of 6 mangoes. Give your answer in dollars and cents.

     6 mangoes cost _____.

2.   Jerry pays $3.75 for some mangoes. How many mangoes does he buy?

     Jerry buys _____ mangoes.

Complete. Use data from the line graph.

The line graph shows the amount of water left in a family's water tank at the end of each day.

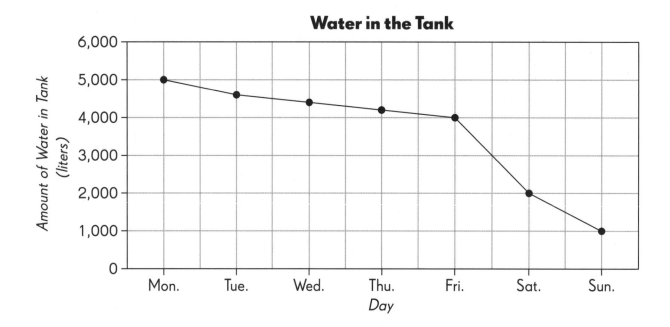

Water in the Tank

3.   How much water was left in the tank on Sunday? _____ liters

4.   What is the difference in the amounts of water left in the tank on

     Friday and on Sunday? _____ liters

5. **a.** Between which two days was the decrease in the amount of water left in the tank the greatest?

Between _____ and _____

b. What was the decrease in the amount of water? _____ liters

6. There are 4 members in the family. Each family member uses the same amount of water. How much water does each family member use from Monday through Sunday?

Each family member uses _____ liters of water.

Complete. Use data from the line graph.

The line graph shows the length of a rubber band when various masses are hung on it.

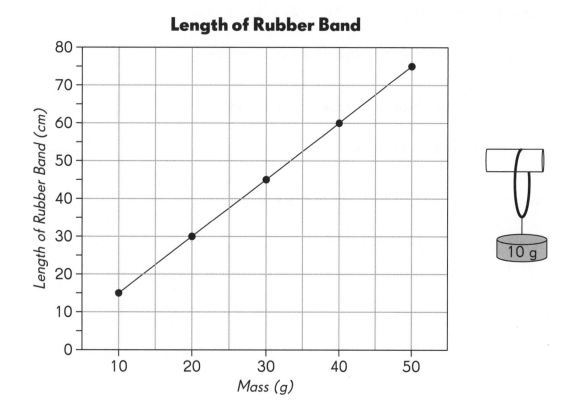

Length of Rubber Band

Example

How much mass is hung on the rubber band when the length of the rubber band is 45 centimeters?

Step 1   Find 45 centimeters along the vertical axis.

Step 2   Move right until you meet a point on the graph.

Step 3   Move down from that point until you meet the horizontal axis.

Step 4   The point on the horizontal axis is 30 grams.

_____30_____ grams is hung on the rubber band.

---

7.   How much mass is hung on the rubber band when

the length of the rubber band is 60 centimeters?   _____

8.   How much mass is hung on the rubber band when

the length of the rubber band is 75 centimeters?   _____

9.   What is the length of the rubber band when

a 10-gram mass is hung on it?   _____

10.   What is the length of the rubber band when

a 20-gram mass is hung on it?   _____

CHAPTER 5 Data and Probability

Worksheet 1   Average

Find the mean or average of each set of data.

Example

The weights of four objects are shown below.

 4 lb   14 lb   24 lb   34 lb

$$\text{Mean or average} = \frac{\text{Total number or amount}}{\text{Number of items}}$$

Step 1   Find the total weight of all the objects.

_____4_____ + _____14_____ + _____24_____ + _____34_____ = __76 lb__

Step 2   Divide the total weight by the number of objects.

_____76_____ ÷ _____4_____ = __19 lb__

The average weight of the four objects is ___19___ pounds.

---

1.   The volumes of five containers are listed below.

48 mL, 26 mL, 32 mL, 57 mL, 97 mL

Step 1   Find the total volume of all the containers.

_____ + _____ + _____ + _____ + _____ = _____ mL

Step 2   Divide the total volume by the number of containers.

_____ ÷ 5 = _____ mL

The average volume of the containers is _____ milliliters.

2. The distances traveled by some trucks are listed below.

536 km, 450 km, 152 km, 824 km, 375 km, 459 km

Total distance = _____ + _____ + _____ + _____ +

_____ + _____

= _____ km

Average distance = _____ ÷ 6 = _____ km

The average distance traveled is _____ kilometers.

Find the total from the mean or average.

> *Example*
>
> The mean length of a side of a square plot of land is 11 meters. What is the plot's perimeter?
>
> Total number or amount
> = Mean or average × Number of items
>
>
>
> A square plot of land has 4 equal sides.
> 11 × 4 = 44 meters
>
> The plot's perimeter is _____44_____ meters.

3. A bottle of milk is poured into 8 smaller cartons. The mean volume of milk in each carton is 375 milliliters. What is the total volume of milk in the cartons?

4. Mrs. Ellis spent an average of $28 on a book. She bought 185 books for the school library. What is the total amount of money Mrs. Ellis spent?

5. Mary walks to school every day. She walks an average distance of 750 meters each day. What is the total distance Mary walked in 5 days?

Total distance Mary walked in 5 days

= _____ × _____ = _____ m

She walked _____ meters in 5 days.

© Marshall Cavendish International (Singapore) Private Limited.

6. The arm lengths of 7 students are measured during a math class. The average length of their arms is 68 centimeters. Find the total length of their arms.

7. The table shows the scores Joe received for four tests.

Test	First	Second	Third	Fourth
Score	67	74	?	92

Joe's mean score for the four tests is 79.

a. Find the total score for the four tests.

b. What is Joe's score for the third test?

Complete. Use the data in the table.

The table shows the number of basketball games that Rudd played in during two years.

Opponent	Number of Games
Dallas	10
Lancaster	9
Chicago	13
Seattle	11
Washington	15

> *Example*
>
> Rudd played _____11_____ games against Seattle.

8. Rudd played the most games against _____.

9. Rudd played a total of _____ games in two years.

10. The average number of games Rudd played a year is _____.

Solve.

Calvin bought 1 kilogram of each type of nut.

> *Example*
>
> How many kilograms of nuts did Calvin buy altogether?
>
> Calvin bought _____ *3* _____ kilograms of nuts altogether.

11.   How much did he pay altogether?

12.   Find the average price of a kilogram of nuts.

Worksheet 2   Median, Mode, and Range

Find the median of each set of data.

Example

4, 7, 9, 12, 16, 25, 33

The median is ____12____.

When a set of data arranged from least to greatest has one middle number, the middle number is the **median**.

1.

(199) (400) (601) (802) (1,003) (1,204) (1,405)

a. What is the middle number? _____

b. What is the median? _____

2.

| 64 kg | 78 kg | 90 kg | 102 kg | 114 kg |

The median mass is _____ kilograms.

3.

Game	A	B	C	D	E
Score	34	46	60	74	88

The median score for the games is _____.

Find the median of each set of data.

> *Example*
>
> | 15 | 25 | 35 | 65 | 85 | 105 |
>
> The two middle numbers are ___35___
>
> and ___65___.
>
> Mean $= \dfrac{35 + 65}{2} = 50$
>
> The median is ___50___.
>
> When a set of data arranged from least to greatest has two middle numbers, the **mean** of these two numbers is the **median**.

4.

| 107 m | 109 m | 111 m | 113 m | 115 m | 117 m |

a. What are the middle numbers?

The middle numbers are _____ and _____.

b. What is the median?

Mean $= \dfrac{\boxed{} + \boxed{}}{2}$

$= \dfrac{\boxed{}}{2}$

$= \boxed{}$ m

The median is _____ meters.

Order each set of data from least to greatest. Then find the median.

Example

These are the sales prices of some electrical appliances in a store.

$42 $15 $23 $33 $10

Ordered from least to greatest:

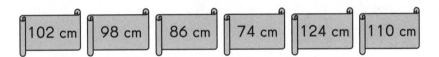

$10 $15 $23 $33 $42

least   greatest

The median price is ___$23___.

5. These are the heights that six students jumped during a high jump event.

102 cm   98 cm   86 cm   74 cm   124 cm   110 cm

Ordered from least to greatest:

least   greatest

The median height is _____ centimeters.

Name: _____ **Date:** _____

Find the mode. Use the data in the line plot.

Harry picks some number cards from a bag. He records the numbers on the line plot. Each **X** represents 1 card.

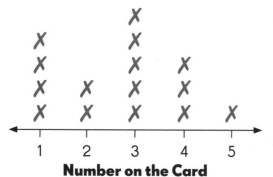

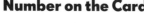

Number on the Card

> *Example*
>
> There are 5 **X**s for the number 3. The number 3 occurs most often.
>
> So, the mode is _____3_____.

> A line plot uses a number line to show data.

> The number that occurs most often is the **mode**.

6. Harry picks out 5 more number cards from the bag. He includes these numbers on the line plot.

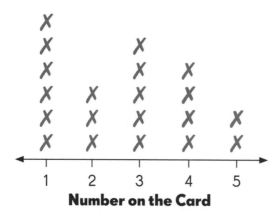

Number on the Card

a. The card with the greatest number of **X**s is _____.

b. The mode of this data set is _____.

c. Harry picked a total of _____ cards from the bag.

Find the modes. Use the data in the line plot.

— *Example* —

Tashi picks 22 number cards from a bag.
She records the numbers on the line plot.

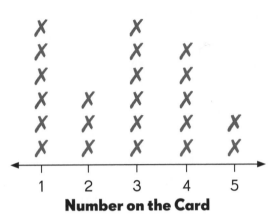

Number on the Card

There are 6 **X**s each for card number 1 and card number 3.

So, the modes of this data set

are ___1 and 3___.

> A set of data can have more than 1 mode.

7. The set of data shows the number of leaves on different branches of a tree.

3, 3, 3, 4, 4, 5, 5, 5, 5, 5, 5, 6, 6, 6, 6, 6, 6, 7, 7, 7, 7, 8, 8, 8, 9, 9

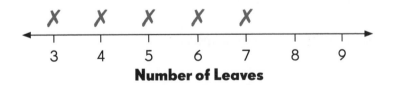

Number of Leaves

a. Complete the line plot. Each **X** represents 1 branch.

b. _____ branches have 7 leaves each.

c. The modes of this data set are _____ and _____.

Find the range of each set of data.

> *Example*
>
> Here are the distances traveled by Mr. Tyler over a two-week period.
>
> 87 miles, 129 miles, 56 miles, 423 miles, 298 miles
>
> > Range = Greatest number − Least number
>
> 423 − 56 = 367 miles
>
> So, the range of this set of numbers is _____367_____ miles.

8. These are the masses a weightlifter lifted during training.

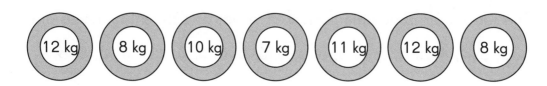

12 kg   8 kg   10 kg   7 kg   11 kg   12 kg   8 kg

   a. The smallest mass is _____.

   b. The largest mass is _____.

   c. The range of the mass lifted

      = largest mass − smallest mass

      = _____ − _____

      = _____

Find the mean of each set of data using a line plot.

Example

Uncle Joe cuts some fruits and counts the number of seeds in each fruit.
The line plot shows the number of seeds in each fruit.
Each ✗ represents 1 fruit.

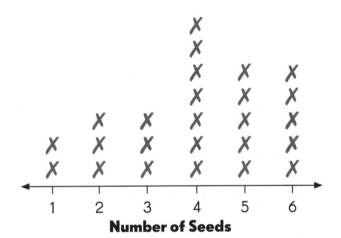

Number of Seeds

2 fruits have 1 seed → 2 × 1 = 2
3 fruits have 2 seeds → 3 × 2 = 6
3 fruits have 3 seeds → 3 × 3 = 9
7 fruits have 4 seeds → 7 × 4 = 28
5 fruits have 5 seeds → 5 × 5 = 25
5 fruits have 6 seeds → 5 × 6 = 30

$$\text{Mean} = \frac{\text{Total number of seeds}}{\text{Total number of fruits}}$$

$$= \frac{2 + 6 + 9 + 28 + 25 + 30}{2 + 3 + 3 + 7 + 5 + 5}$$

$$= \frac{100}{25} = 4$$

The mean number of seeds is _____4_____.

9.   The line plot shows the lengths of ribbon Mrs. Kent cut.

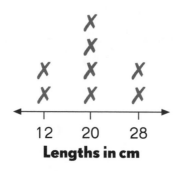

Lengths in cm

2 ribbons have a length of 12 centimeters ➜ 2 × 12 = ☐ cm

4 ribbons have a length of 20 centimeters ➜ 4 × 20 = ☐ cm

2 ribbons have a length of 28 centimeters ➜ 2 × 28 = ☐ cm

Total length of all the ribbons = ☐ + ☐ + ☐

= ☐ cm

$$\text{Mean} = \frac{\text{Total length of ribbons}}{\text{Total number of ribbons}} = \frac{\boxed{}}{\boxed{}}$$

= ☐ cm

The mean length of the ribbons is _____ centimeters.

10. Students were asked to count the number of marbles in their marble bags. The table shows the data collected.

Number of Bags	6	10	4	8	7
Number of Marbles in Each Bag	5	6	7	8	9

Make a line plot to show the data. Each X represents 1 bag.

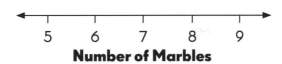

Number of Marbles

☐ bags have 5 marbles each → ☐ × ☐

= ☐

☐ bags have 6 marbles each → ☐ × ☐

= ☐

☐ bags have 7 marbles each → ☐ × ☐

= ☐

☐ bags have 8 marbles each ➜ ☐ × ☐

= ☐

☐ bags have 9 marbles each ➜ ☐ × ☐

= ☐

Total number of marbles = ☐ + ☐ + ☐ + ☐ + ☐

= ☐

$$\text{Mean} = \frac{\text{Total number of marbles}}{\text{Total number of bags}} = \frac{\boxed{}}{\boxed{}}$$

= ☐

The mean number of marbles is _____.

Solve. Show your work.

Uncle Sam visits some houses to find out the number of people living in each house. The line plot shows the number of houses and the number of people living in each house. Each ✗ represents 1 house.

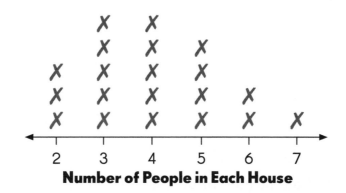

Number of People in Each House

11. What is the range of the number of people living in the houses?

12. How many houses in the survey have only 2 people living in them?

13. How many houses in the survey have the greatest number of people living in them?

14. Find the mean of the number of people living in each house.

15. Find the modes of this set of data.

Worksheet 3   Stem-and-Leaf Plots

Complete.

These are the scores students received in a math quiz.

67, 42, 73, 75, 88, 94, 69, 97, 81, 98

Example

Make a stem-and-leaf plot with the given set of data.

Step 1   Order the scores from least to greatest.

42, 67, 69, 73, 75, 81, 88, 94, 97, 98

Step 2   Put the tens digits in the stem column.

Step 3   Put the ones digits in the leaves column.

Place the tens digits in the stem column.

outlier

Math Quiz Scores	
Stem	**Leaves**
4	2
6	7 9
7	3 5
8	1 8
9	4 7 8

Order the numbers in the ones place from least to greatest.

6|7 stands for _____67_____.

---

1.   The outlier of a data set is the number farthest away from the rest of the

data. The outlier of this set of data is _____.

2.   The stem 9 has _____ leaves.

Complete.

These are the number of rolls that Sally's bakery sold on different days during the month of October.

52   27   48   24   34   41   58   45   47   63

3.   Order the number of rolls from least to greatest.

_____

4.   Complete the stem-and-leaf plot.

Number of Rolls	
Stem	Leaves
2	
3	
4	
5	
6	

5.   **a.**   The stem 3 has _____ leaves.

b.   2 | 4 stands for _____.

c.   The greatest number of rolls sold is _____.

d.   Altogether, there are _____ leaves in this set of data.

© Marshall Cavendish International (Singapore) Private Limited.

Find the median, mode, and range. Use the stem-and-leaf plot.

The stem-and-leaf plot shows the weight of the apples sold at a market.

Weight of Apples (lb)	
Stem	Leaves
3	2 7
4	5 6 6 9
5	3 3 8 8
6	0 2 5 7 9
7	1 2 4 5
9	6

3 | 2 stands for ___32___ .

Example

The median weight is ___?___ .

Median $= \dfrac{58 + 60}{2} = \dfrac{118}{2} = 59$ lb

The median weight is ___59___ pounds.

> Since there are 20 leaves, the set of data has two middle numbers. The two middle numbers are 58 and 60.
---

6. **a.** The modes are the numbers that occur most often. So, the modes are

_____, _____, and _____.

b. Range = Greatest number − Least number

= _____ lb − 32 lb

= _____ lb

c. The outlier in this set of data is _____ pounds.

Complete the sentences. Use the data in the stem-and-leaf plot.

The stem-and-leaf plot shows the length of some snakes measured in centimeters.

Length of Snakes (cm)	
Stem	**Leaves**
2	1 6 7
3	4 5 5 8
4	2 2 2 4 6 7 7
5	0 1 4 6
6	1 5

2 | 1 stands for _____21_____.

> **Example**
>
> The length that appears most often is _____42_____ centimeters.

7. **a.** The mode of the set of data is _____ centimeters.

    b. 3 | 4 stands for _____ centimeters.

    c. The length of the longest snake is _____ centimeters.

    d. The length of the shortest snake is _____ centimeters.

    e. The range of the lengths is _____ centimeters.

    f. The median length of the snakes is _____ centimeters.

Complete. Show your work.

The table shows the amount of money each stall collected during the fair.

Stall	Amount of Money
A	$42
B	$59
C	$46
D	$60
E	$64
F	$75
G	$79
H	$68
I	$65

> **Example**
>
> Which stall collected the most amount of money? _____ *Stall G* _____

8.   **a.**   Make a stem-and-leaf plot to show the set of data.

Amount of Money	
Stem	**Leaves**

4 | 2 stands for 42.

b. Is there a mode for this set of data? Explain your answer.

_____

_____

c. What is the range of the amount of money collected?

Range = Greatest amount − Least amount

       = _____ − _____

       = _____

The range of the amount of money collected is _____.

d. Find the median amount of money collected.

The median amount of money collected is _____.

e. What is the total amount of money collected at the fair?

A total of _____ was collected.

f. Find the average amount of money collected by each stall.

Average amount of money collected

$$= \frac{\text{Total amount of money collected}}{\text{Number of stalls}}$$

$$= \frac{\boxed{}}{\boxed{}} = \boxed{}$$

The average amount of money collected by each stall is _____.

Worksheet 4   Outcomes

Describe the likelihood of each outcome. Write *more likely*, *less likely*, *equally likely*, *certain*, or *impossible*.

There are 2 red marbles and 4 blue marbles in a bag. One marble is drawn from the bag at a time.

Example

A red marble will be drawn from the bag.   _____less likely_____

Since there are fewer red marbles than blue marbles, it is less likely that a red marble will be drawn.

---

1.   A blue marble will be drawn.   _____

2.   After two blue marbles are removed from the bag,

a red marble will be drawn.   _____

3.   Four yellow marbles are now added to the bag in Exercise 2.

a.   A yellow marble will be drawn.   _____

b.   A blue marble will be drawn.   _____

4.   All the red and blue marbles are removed from the bag in Exercise 3.

a.   A yellow marble will be drawn.   _____

b.   A green marble will be drawn.   _____

Find the possible outcomes. Then describe each likelihood using
more likely, less likely, equally likely, certain, or *impossible.*

Look at the spinners. Each spinner is spun once.

Example

Possible Outcome	Yellow
Likelihood of Landing on Yellow	Certain

5.

Possible Outcome	
Likelihood of Landing on Yellow	

6.

Possible Outcome	
Likelihood of Landing on Yellow	

7.

Green Green / Green Green

Possible Outcome	
Likelihood of Landing on Yellow	

Check (✔) the correct statement that describes each possible outcome.

All the cubes are put into a bag and a cube is drawn from the bag.

Example

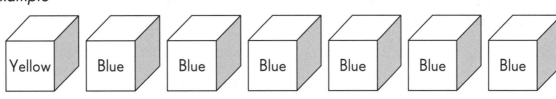

a. You are more likely to draw a yellow cube than a blue cube. ☐

b. You are more likely to draw a blue cube than a yellow cube.

8.

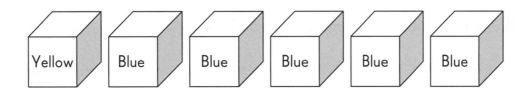

a. You are less likely to draw a yellow cube than a blue cube. ☐

b. You are less likely to draw a blue cube than a yellow cube. ☐

9.

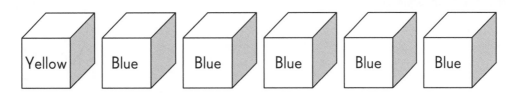

a. It is impossible to draw a yellow cube. ☐

b. It is impossible to draw a green cube. ☐

10.

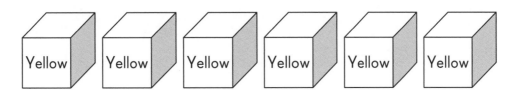

a. It is certain that you will draw a yellow cube. ☐

b. It is certain that you will draw a blue cube. ☐

Read each description of the outcome. Then label the color of the parts of the spinner.

Each spinner is divided into 8 equal parts. Use *B* to represent blue and *Y* to represent yellow.

Example

It is more likely that the spinner will land on blue than on yellow.

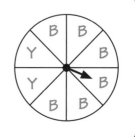

---

11. It is impossible for the spinner to land on blue.

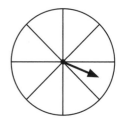

12. It is as equally likely that the spinner will land on blue as on yellow.

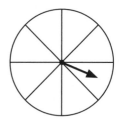

13. It is certain that the spinner will land on blue.

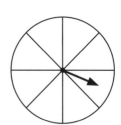

© Marshall Cavendish International (Singapore) Private Limited.

Worksheet 5   Probability as a Fraction

Find the probability as a fraction in simplest form.

Shawn made a spinner with 6 equal parts. He labeled each part with the numbers 1 through 6. Shawn spins the spinner once.

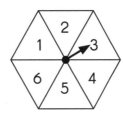

Example

Find the probability of landing on 2 or 3.

Step 1   Find the number of favorable outcomes.

There are only ____2____ favorable outcomes.

Step 2   Find the total number of possible outcomes.

There are ____6____ possible outcomes.

Step 3   Find the probability as a fraction.

Probability of a favorable outcome

$= \dfrac{\text{Number of favorable outcomes}}{\text{Total number of possible outcomes}} = \dfrac{2}{6} = \dfrac{1}{3}$

The probability of landing on 2 or 3 is ____$\dfrac{1}{3}$____.

> A favorable outcome is the result you want.

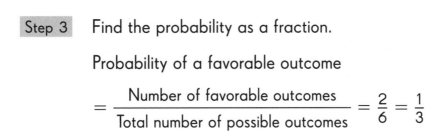

1.   The probability of landing on an odd number.

The odd numbers are _____, _____, and _____.

Number of favorable outcomes = _____

Number of possible outcomes = 6

Probability of landing on an odd number

$$= \frac{\text{Number of favorable outcomes}}{\text{Total number of possible outcomes}} = \frac{\boxed{}}{6} = \frac{\boxed{}}{\boxed{}}$$

The probability of landing on an odd number is _____.

2.   The probability of landing on a number less than 5.

The numbers less than 5 are _____, _____, _____, and _____.

Number of favorable outcomes = _____

Number of possible outcomes = _____

Probability of landing on a number less than 5

$$= \frac{\text{Number of favorable outcomes}}{\text{Total number of possible outcomes}} = \frac{\boxed{}}{6} = \frac{\boxed{}}{\boxed{}}$$

The probability of landing on a number less than 5 is _____.

3. The probability of landing on a number greater than 3.

The numbers greater than 3 are _____, _____, and _____.

Number of favorable outcomes = _____

Number of possible outcomes = _____

Probability of landing on a number greater than 3

$$= \frac{\text{Number of favorable outcomes}}{\text{Total number of possible outcomes}} = \frac{\boxed{}}{\boxed{}} = \frac{\boxed{}}{\boxed{}}$$

The probability of landing on a number greater than 3 is _____.

Find each probability on the number line as a fraction in simplest form. Then describe the probability of each outcome as *certain*, *impossible*, *more likely*, *less likely*, or *equally likely*.

There are 5 red cubes, 3 green cubes, and 2 yellow cubes in a bag. One cube is drawn from the bag.

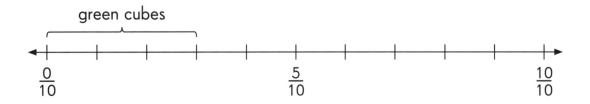

green cubes

$\frac{0}{10}$ $\frac{5}{10}$ $\frac{10}{10}$

Example

The probability of drawing a green cube is ____$\frac{3}{10}$____.

The number line shows that the likelihood of this outcome is

____*less likely*____ as $\frac{3}{10}$ is nearer to $\frac{0}{10}$ than to $\frac{10}{10}$.

> The closer the probability of an outcome is to 1, the more likely the outcome is to occur.

---

4. The probability of drawing a red cube.

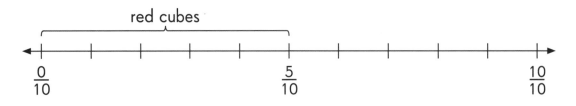

red cubes

$\frac{0}{10}$ $\frac{5}{10}$ $\frac{10}{10}$

Probability: $\dfrac{\square}{\square} = \dfrac{\square}{\square}$ Likelihood of outcome: _____

5.   The probability of drawing a yellow cube.

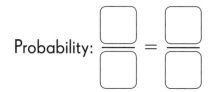

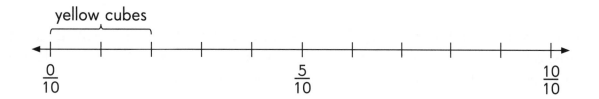

Probability: ⬜/⬜ = ⬜/⬜   Likelihood of outcome: _____

6.   The probability of drawing a red cube or a yellow cube.

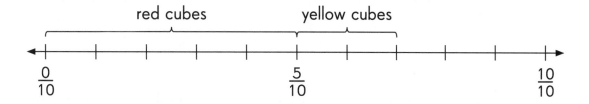

Probability: ⬜/⬜   Likelihood of outcome: _____

7.   The probability of drawing a blue cube.

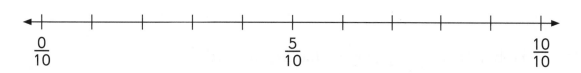

Probability: ⬜/⬜ = ⬜   Likelihood of outcome: _____

Name: _____ **Date:** _____

Find the probability of each outcome. Then describe the outcome as *certain, impossible, more likely, less likely,* or *equally likely.*

Joyce has a set of 10 animal cards. There are 5 dog cards, 2 cat cards, 2 rabbit cards, and 1 bird card in the set. She shuffles the cards, places them face down in a stack, and draws the first card from the top of the stack.

Example

Probability of a dog card $= \dfrac{5}{10} = \dfrac{1}{2}$

It is ___equally likely___ to draw a dog card.

---

8. Probability of a rabbit card $= \dfrac{\square}{\square} = \dfrac{\square}{\square}$ Likelihood of outcome: _____

9. Probability of a dog or a cat card $= \dfrac{\square}{\square}$ Likelihood of outcome: _____

10. Probability of a cat, rabbit, or a bird card $= \dfrac{\square}{\square} = \dfrac{\square}{\square}$

Likelihood of outcome: _____

11. Probability of a dog, cat, rabbit, or bird card $= \dfrac{\square}{\square} = \square$

Likelihood of outcome: _____

12. Probability of a mouse card $= \dfrac{\square}{\square} = \square$ Likelihood of outcome: _____

Worksheet 6   Real-World Problems: Data and Probability

Solve each problem using the mean. Show your work.

Example

The mean weight of 3 sisters is 92 pounds.
The total weight of 2 of the sisters is 178 pounds.
Find the weight of the third sister.

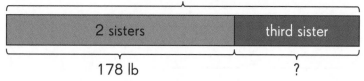

3 × 92 lb = 276 lb

| 2 sisters | third sister |

178 lb   ?

Total weight = 3 × mean weight = 3 × 92 lb = 276 lb
Weight of the third sister = Total weight − 178 lb
$$= 276 \text{ lb} - 178 \text{ lb}$$
$$= 98 \text{ lb}$$

The weight of the third sister is ____98____ pounds.

---

1.   The mean income of 4 workers is $1,250.
The total income of 3 of the workers is $3,420.
Find the income of the fourth worker.

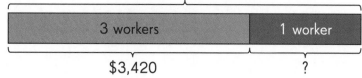

Total income of 4 workers

| 3 workers | 1 worker |

$3,420   ?

Total income of 4 workers = 4 × mean income

$$= 4 \times \underline{\hspace{1.5cm}} = \underline{\hspace{1.5cm}}$$

Income of 3 workers = $3,420

Income of the 4th worker = \underline{\hspace{1.5cm}} − \underline{\hspace{1.5cm}} = \underline{\hspace{1.5cm}}

The income of the 4th worker is $\underline{\hspace{1.5cm}}.

2. The total cost of 10 toys is $780.
The mean cost of 3 of the toys is $40.
The mean cost of 5 of the other toys is $50.
Find the mean cost of the remaining 2 toys.

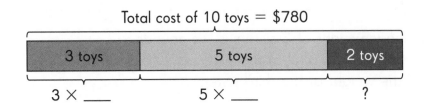

Cost of 3 toys = 3 × _____ = _____

Cost of 5 toys = 5 × _____ = _____

Cost of 8 toys = _____ + _____ = _____

Cost of the remaining 2 toys = _____ − _____ = _____

Mean cost of the 2 toys = $\dfrac{\boxed{}}{2}$ = _____

The mean cost of the remaining 2 toys is $_____.

3. The mean mass of a goat and a sheep is 78 kilograms.
The sheep is 6 kilograms heavier than the goat.
Find the mass of each animal.

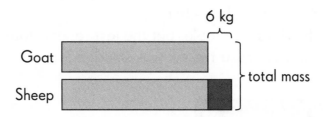

Total mass of the goat and sheep

= 2 × _____

= _____

2 units → Total mass − _____

         = _____ − _____

         = _____

1 unit → $\dfrac{\boxed{}}{2}$ = _____

The mass of the goat is _____ kilograms.

_____ + 6 kg = _____

The mass of the sheep is _____ kilograms.

**Solve each problem to find the mean, median, mode, and range.
Show your work.**

4.   A gardener delivered roses to 6 florists.
        He delivered 684 roses altogether.
        He recorded the data in a table, but the last row of data
        could not be read because the ink was smudged.

Florist	Number of Roses
A	108
B	156
C	96
D	120
E	84
F	?

> *Example*
>
> Find the mean number of
> roses he delivered.
>
> Mean $= \dfrac{684}{6} = 114$
>
> The mean number of roses
> he delivered is ____114____.

a.   How many roses did he deliver to Florist F?

Number of roses delivered to 5 florists

= _____ + _____ + _____ + _____ + _____

= _____

Number of roses delivered to Florist F

= Total number of roses − _____

= _____ − _____

= _____

The number of roses he delivered to Florist F is _____.

b.   Find the range of the number of roses he delivered.

Range = Greatest number − Least number

= _____ − _____

= _____

The range of the number of roses delivered is _____.

c.   Find the mode of the set of data.

The mode of the set of data is _____.

d.   Find the median of the set of data.

Order the numbers from least to greatest.

The middle numbers are _____ and _____.

Mean = $\dfrac{\boxed{} + \boxed{}}{2} = \boxed{}$

The median of the set of data is _____.

5.   In a javelin competition, Sam threw the javelin 5 times. The table shows the distance the javelin traveled on each throw. The recorder misplaced 2 of the 5 readings.

Throw	1	2	3	4	5
Distance	68 m	72 m	66 m	?	?

Help the recorder to find the two missing readings using this information.

The range of the data is 8 meters.
The shortest distance thrown is 66 meters.
The mean distance thrown is 70 meters.

a.   Find the longest distance the javelin was thrown.

Range = Longest distance − Shortest distance

Longest distance = _____ + _____ = _____

The longest distance the javelin was thrown is _____ meters.

b.   Find the missing data.

Total distance
= mean distance × number of throws

> Use average or mean to find the total.

= _____ × 5 = _____

The missing data
= total distance − distance of the 4 throws

= _____ − 68 m − 72 m − 66 m − _____

= _____

The missing data is _____ meters.

c.   Find the median distance of the 5 throws.

Order the distances from least to greatest.

The median distance is _____ meters.

Name: _____ **Date:** _____

Solve each problem using a stem-and-leaf plot.

6. Mr. Williams deposits money in his bank account once a month for 12 months.

Amount of Money	
Stem	**Leaves**
6	3 6 8
7	2 ?
8	0 4 4 9
9	1 2 7

6 | 3 stands for ____63____

Example

The mean amount of money he deposits each month is $80.
Find the total amount of money he deposits in 12 months.

Total amount of money = Mean × Number of months
                      = $80 × 12
                      = $960

He deposits ____$960____ in 12 months.

---

a. Find the missing data in stem 7.

Total amount − Amount of money deposited in 11 months

= ⬚ − ⬚ − ⬚ − ⬚ − ⬚ − ⬚ − ⬚ −

⬚ − ⬚ − ⬚ − ⬚ − ⬚ = ⬚

The missing data in stem 7 is $_____.

b. The mode of the set of data is _____.

c. The median of the set of data is _____.

d. The range of the set of data is _____.

Solve. Show your work.

7.   The line plot shows the weight of watermelons (rounded to the nearest pound) sold at a supermarket. Each **X** represents 1 watermelon.

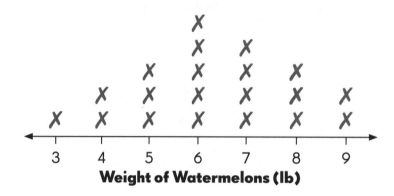

Weight of Watermelons (lb)

a.   The mode of the set of data is _____ pounds.

b.   The median weight of the watermelons is _____ pounds.

c.   Each pound of watermelon costs $3. What is the total cost of all the watermelons?

The total cost of all the watermelons is $_____.

Solve each problem by finding the probability or by describing the outcome. Show your work.

8. A bag contains 16 marbles.
6 marbles are red, 5 are blue, 3 are green, and 2 are yellow.

Example

Sylvia draws 1 marble from the bag.
What is the probability that the marble is red?

Number of favorable outcomes = 6
Number of possible outcomes = 16

Probability of drawing a red marble = $\frac{6}{16}$ = $\frac{3}{8}$

The probability that the marble is red is ___$\frac{3}{8}$___.

---

a. Sylvia returns the red marble to the bag. Then she draws 2 marbles from the bag, one at a time. Describe the outcome as *certain*, *impossible*, *more likely*, *less likely*, or *equally likely*.

i. It is _____ that the first marble is yellow.

ii. If the first marble is green, it is _____ that the second marble is yellow or green.

iii. If the first marble is red, it is _____ that the second marble is red, yellow, or green.

iv. If the first marble is blue, it is _____ that the second marble is red, blue, green, or yellow.

b. Sylvia returns the 2 marbles to the bag, and Tyron adds 1 blue marble and 3 green marbles to the bag. He then draws 1 marble from the bag. Find the probability as a fraction in simplest form.

i. What is the probability that a red marble is drawn?

Number of favorable outcomes = _____

Number of possible outcomes = 16 + 1 + 3 = _____

Probability of drawing a red marble

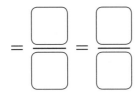

The probability that a red marble is drawn is _____.

ii. What is the probability that Tyron draws a red, blue, or green marble?

Number of favorable outcomes = _____

Number of possible outcomes = _____

Probability of drawing a red, blue, or green marble

$= \dfrac{\boxed{}}{\boxed{}} = \dfrac{\boxed{}}{\boxed{}}$

The probability that Tyron draws a red, blue, or green

marble is _____.

CHAPTER 6 Fractions and Mixed Numbers

Worksheet 1   Adding Fractions

Find the equivalent fraction. Shade the models.

Example

$\frac{2}{3}$

?

$$\frac{2}{3} = \frac{6}{9}$$

1. $\frac{1}{2}$

?

$$\frac{1}{2} = \frac{\square}{\square}$$

2. $\frac{3}{5}$

?

$$\frac{3}{5} = \frac{\square}{\square}$$

Find the equivalent fractions.

Example

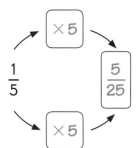

To get the equivalent fraction, multiply both the numerator and the denominator by the same number.

3.

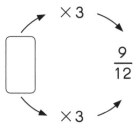

4.

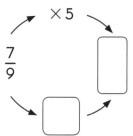

5.

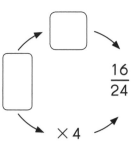

6.

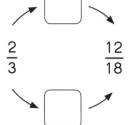

Find the equivalent fractions. Complete the model by shading the correct number of parts. Then add the fractions.

Example

$\frac{1}{3} + \frac{2}{9} = ?$

Step 1   Change the denominator of $\frac{1}{3}$ to 9.

$\frac{1}{3} = \boxed{\frac{3}{9}}$

$\frac{1}{3} \overset{\times 3}{=} \boxed{\frac{3}{9}} \overset{\times 3}{}$

Step 2   Add the like fractions.

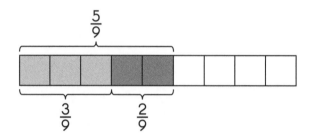

$\frac{3}{9}$ $\frac{2}{9}$

$\frac{1}{3} + \frac{2}{9} = \boxed{\frac{3}{9}} + \frac{2}{9} = \boxed{\frac{5}{9}}$

7. $\frac{3}{8} + \frac{1}{4}$

$\frac{1}{4} \overset{\boxed{}}{=} \boxed{} \overset{\times 2}{}$

$\frac{1}{4} = \boxed{}$

$\frac{3}{8} + \frac{1}{4} = \frac{3}{8} + \boxed{}$

$= \boxed{}$

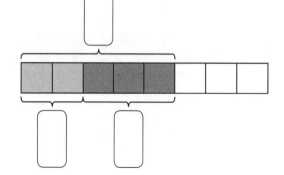

8. $\dfrac{1}{12} + \dfrac{1}{3}$

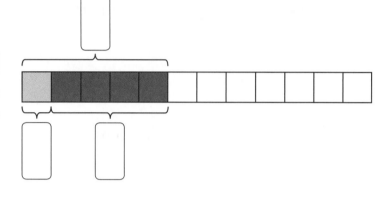

$\dfrac{1}{3} = \boxed{}$

$\dfrac{1}{3} = \boxed{}$

$\dfrac{1}{12} + \dfrac{1}{3} = \boxed{} + \boxed{}$

$= \boxed{}$

Complete the models. Then add the fractions.

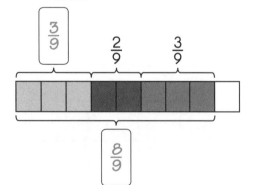

Example

$\dfrac{1}{3} + \dfrac{2}{9} + \dfrac{3}{9} = ?$

$\dfrac{1}{3} = \boxed{\dfrac{3}{9}}$

$\dfrac{1}{3} \quad = \quad \boxed{\dfrac{3}{9}} \qquad \times 3$

$\dfrac{1}{3} + \dfrac{2}{9} + \dfrac{3}{9} = \boxed{\dfrac{3}{9}} + \dfrac{2}{9} + \dfrac{3}{9}$

$= \boxed{\dfrac{8}{9}}$

So, $\dfrac{1}{3} + \dfrac{2}{9} + \dfrac{3}{9} = \dfrac{8}{9}$.

9. $\dfrac{1}{8} + \dfrac{1}{2} + \dfrac{3}{8}$

$\dfrac{1}{2} = \boxed{}$

$\dfrac{1}{2} \begin{array}{c} \xrightarrow{\times 4} \\ = \\ \xrightarrow{\times 4} \end{array} \boxed{}$

$\boxed{}$

$\overset{\dfrac{1}{8}}{} \qquad \overset{\dfrac{3}{8}}{}$

$\boxed{}$

$\dfrac{1}{8} + \dfrac{1}{2} + \dfrac{3}{8} = \dfrac{1}{8} + \boxed{} + \dfrac{3}{8}$

$= \boxed{}$

$= \boxed{}$

10. $\dfrac{1}{12} + \dfrac{1}{4} + \dfrac{5}{12}$

$\boxed{} \quad \boxed{} \qquad \boxed{}$

$\dfrac{1}{4} = \boxed{}$

$\boxed{}$

$\dfrac{1}{12} + \dfrac{1}{4} + \dfrac{5}{12} = \boxed{} + \boxed{} + \boxed{}$

$= \boxed{}$

$= \boxed{}$

Express each fraction in simplest form.

Example

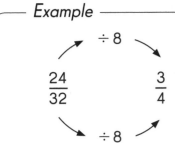

$$\frac{24}{32} \quad \overset{\div 8}{\underset{\div 8}{\longrightarrow}} \quad \frac{3}{4}$$

To simplify a fraction, divide both the numerator and the denominator by the same number.

$$\frac{24}{32} = \frac{\boxed{3}}{\boxed{4}}$$

11. $\dfrac{12}{34} = \dfrac{\boxed{}}{\boxed{}}$

12. $\dfrac{18}{42} = \dfrac{\boxed{}}{\boxed{}}$

A fraction is in its simplest form when the numerator and the denominator cannot both be divided by the same number.

13. $\dfrac{21}{63} = \dfrac{\boxed{}}{\boxed{}}$

Add. Express each answer in simplest form.

Example

$$\frac{2}{5} + \frac{1}{5} = ?$$

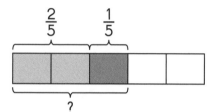

To add like fractions, add the numerators.

So, $\frac{2}{5} + \frac{1}{5} = \dfrac{\boxed{3}}{\boxed{5}}$.

14. $\frac{2}{7} + \frac{3}{7} = \dfrac{\boxed{}}{\boxed{}}$

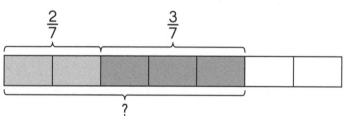

15. $\frac{2}{9} + \frac{4}{9} = \dfrac{\boxed{}}{\boxed{}}$

$= \dfrac{\boxed{}}{\boxed{}}$

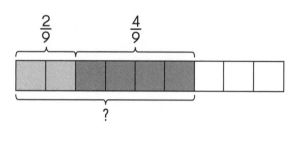

16. $\frac{5}{12} + \frac{7}{12} = \dfrac{\boxed{}}{\boxed{}}$

$= \boxed{}$

17. $\dfrac{3}{10} + \dfrac{2}{5} + \dfrac{1}{10}$

$= \dfrac{3}{10} + \boxed{} + \dfrac{1}{10}$

$\dfrac{2}{5} = $ (circle diagram with boxes)

$= \boxed{}$

$= \boxed{}$

18. $\dfrac{1}{4} + \dfrac{1}{6} + \dfrac{5}{12} = \boxed{} + \boxed{} + \dfrac{5}{12}$

$= \boxed{}$

$\dfrac{1}{4} = $ (circle diagram) $\dfrac{1}{6} = $ (circle diagram)

$= \boxed{}$

Worksheet 2   Subtracting Fractions

Find the equivalent fraction. Complete the model by shading the correct number of parts.

___ *Example* ___

$\frac{2}{3} = \dfrac{\boxed{6}}{\boxed{9}}$

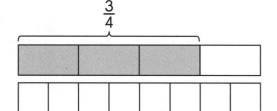

$\frac{2}{3}$

$\frac{6}{9}$

1.

$\frac{3}{4}$

$\dfrac{3}{4} = \dfrac{\boxed{}}{\boxed{}}$

2.

$\frac{2}{5}$

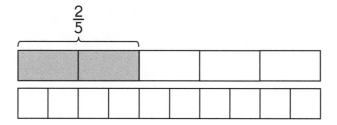

$\dfrac{2}{5} = \dfrac{\boxed{}}{\boxed{}}$

Subtract. Express each answer in simplest form.

Example

$$\frac{5}{6} - \frac{3}{6} = \boxed{\frac{2}{6}} = \boxed{\frac{1}{3}}$$

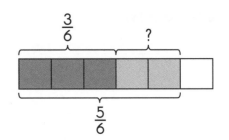

To subtract like fractions, subtract the numerators.

3. $\frac{5}{8} - \frac{3}{8} = \boxed{} = \boxed{}$

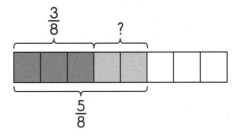

4. $\frac{9}{10} - \frac{7}{10} = \boxed{} = \boxed{}$

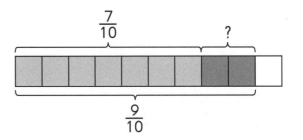

5. $\frac{7}{12} - \frac{4}{12} = \boxed{} = \boxed{}$

Complete the models by shading the correct number of parts.
Then subtract the fractions.

Example

$$\frac{7}{8} - \frac{3}{4} = ?$$

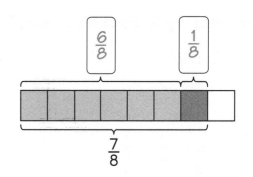

Step 1   Change the denominator of $\frac{3}{4}$ to 8,

so that it has the same denominator as $\frac{7}{8}$.

Step 2   Subtract the like fractions.

$$\frac{7}{8} - \frac{3}{4} = \frac{7}{8} - \boxed{\frac{6}{8}} = \boxed{\frac{1}{8}}$$

So, $\frac{7}{8} - \frac{3}{4} = \frac{1}{8}$.

6. $\dfrac{11}{12} - \dfrac{3}{4}$

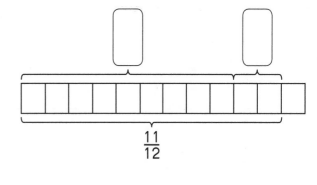

$$\frac{3}{4} = \boxed{}$$

$$\frac{11}{12} - \frac{3}{4} = \frac{11}{12} - \boxed{} = \boxed{}$$

$$= \boxed{}$$

7. $1 - \dfrac{5}{9}$

$1 = \boxed{}$

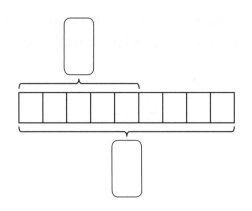

$1 - \dfrac{5}{9} = \boxed{} - \dfrac{5}{9} = \boxed{}$

Find the equivalent fractions. Then subtract.

Example

$\dfrac{7}{9} - \dfrac{2}{3} = \,?$

$\dfrac{7}{9} - \dfrac{2}{3} = \dfrac{7}{9} - \boxed{\dfrac{6}{9}}$

$\dfrac{2}{3} \quad \overset{\times 3}{\underset{\times 3}{=}} \quad \boxed{\dfrac{6}{9}}$

$= \boxed{\dfrac{1}{9}}$

So, $\dfrac{7}{9} - \dfrac{2}{3} = \dfrac{1}{9}$.

---

8. $1 - \dfrac{7}{10} = \boxed{} - \dfrac{7}{10}$

$\dfrac{1}{1} \quad \overset{\times 10}{\underset{\times 10}{=}} \quad \boxed{}$

$= \boxed{}$

9. $\frac{7}{12} - \frac{1}{4} = \frac{7}{12} - \boxed{}$

$= \boxed{}$

$= \boxed{}$

$\frac{1}{4}$ $=$

10. $\frac{11}{12} - \frac{1}{6} = \frac{11}{12} - \boxed{}$

$= \boxed{}$

$= \boxed{}$

$\frac{1}{6}$ $=$

Name: _____ **Date:** _____

Complete the models. Then subtract.

Example

$$1 - \frac{2}{9} - \frac{1}{3} = \text{?}$$

$$1 - \frac{2}{9} - \frac{1}{3}$$

$$= \boxed{\frac{9}{9}} - \frac{2}{9} - \boxed{\frac{3}{9}} = \boxed{\frac{4}{9}}$$

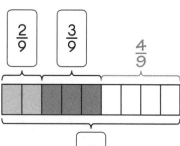

So, $1 - \frac{2}{9} - \frac{1}{3} = \frac{4}{9}$.

---

11. $1 - \frac{4}{12} - \frac{1}{4}$

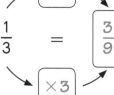

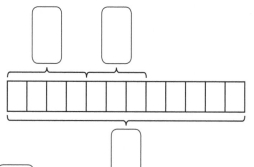

$$1 - \frac{4}{12} - \frac{1}{4} = \boxed{} - \frac{4}{12} - \boxed{} = \boxed{}$$

12. $1 - \frac{2}{10} - \frac{3}{5}$

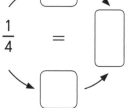

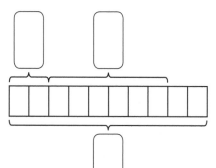

$$1 - \frac{2}{10} - \frac{3}{5} = \boxed{} - \boxed{} - \boxed{} = \boxed{} = \boxed{}$$

Find each difference. Express your answer in simplest form.

Example

$1 - \dfrac{2}{9} - \dfrac{1}{3} = ?$

$1 - \dfrac{2}{9} - \dfrac{1}{3}$

$= \boxed{\dfrac{9}{9}} - \dfrac{2}{9} - \boxed{\dfrac{3}{9}}$

$= \boxed{\dfrac{4}{9}}$

$\dfrac{1}{3} \xrightarrow{\times 3} \boxed{\dfrac{3}{9}}$ (with ×3 on bottom)

So, $1 - \dfrac{2}{9} - \dfrac{1}{3} = \dfrac{4}{9}$.

13. $\dfrac{17}{21} - \dfrac{2}{3} = \dfrac{17}{21} - \boxed{}$

$= \boxed{}$

$= \boxed{}$

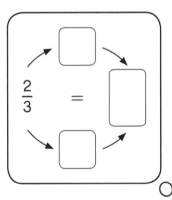

$\dfrac{2}{3} = \boxed{}$

14. $1 - \dfrac{1}{4} - \dfrac{5}{12} = \boxed{} - \boxed{} - \dfrac{5}{12}$

$= \boxed{}$

$= \boxed{}$

15. $1 - \dfrac{1}{4} - \dfrac{3}{20} = \boxed{} - \boxed{} - \dfrac{3}{20}$

$= \boxed{}$

$= \boxed{}$

Worksheet 3 Mixed Numbers

Shade the model to show each mixed number.

Example

$2 + \frac{1}{3} = ?$

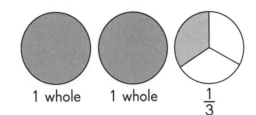

1 whole   1 whole $\frac{1}{3}$

So, $2 + \frac{1}{3} =$ _____ $2\frac{1}{3}$.

When you add a whole number and a fraction, you get a **mixed number**. $2\frac{1}{3}$ is a mixed number.

1.

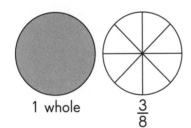

1 whole $\frac{3}{8}$

$\boxed{} + \boxed{} = 1\frac{3}{8}$

2.

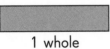 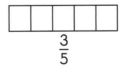

1 whole   1 whole $\frac{3}{5}$

$\boxed{} + \boxed{} = 2\frac{3}{5}$

Find the mixed number that describes each model.

Example

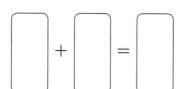

1 whole   1 whole   4 ninths

$$2 + \boxed{\dfrac{4}{9}} = \boxed{2\dfrac{4}{9}}$$

3.

1 whole   1 whole   1 whole   3 fifths

$$\boxed{} + \boxed{} = \boxed{}$$

4.

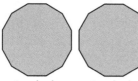 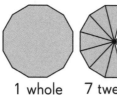

1 whole   1 whole   7 twelfths

$$\boxed{} + \boxed{} = \boxed{}$$

Write each mixed number on the number line.

Example

$1\dfrac{1}{2}$

$1\dfrac{1}{2}$

$$\begin{array}{c|c|c|c}
+ & | & | & | \rightarrow \\
0 & & 1 & 2
\end{array}$$

5. $1\frac{1}{3}$ **6.** $2\frac{2}{3}$ **7.** $3\frac{2}{3}$

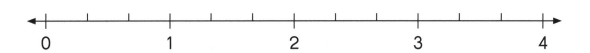

Express each mixed number in simplest form.

Example

$1\frac{2}{4} = ?$

Method 1
Draw models.

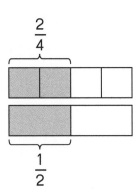

$\frac{2}{4}$

$\frac{1}{2}$

So, $1\frac{2}{4} = 1\frac{1}{2}$.

Method 2
Divide the numerator and the denominator by the same number.

$$\frac{2}{4} \;\overset{\div 2}{\underset{\div 2}{=}}\; \frac{1}{2}$$

So, $1\frac{2}{4} = 1\frac{1}{2}$.

8. $2\frac{3}{12}$ **9.** $3\frac{6}{8}$

Name: _____ **Date:** _____

Find the number of wholes and parts that are shaded. Then write each sum as a mixed number in simplest form.

Example

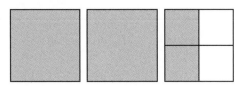

$$2 + \boxed{\dfrac{2}{4}} = \boxed{2\dfrac{2}{4}} = \boxed{2\dfrac{1}{2}}$$

10.

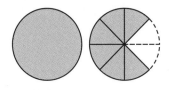

$$1 + \boxed{} = \boxed{}$$

$$= \boxed{}$$

11.

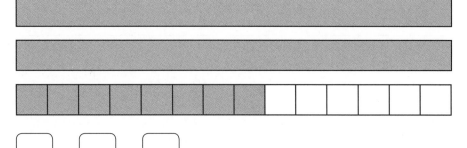

$$\boxed{} + \boxed{} = \boxed{}$$

$$= \boxed{}$$

Name: _____   Date: _____

Worksheet 4   Improper Fractions

Write each description as a fraction.

> *Example*
>
> 1 third = $\boxed{\dfrac{1}{3}}$

1.   3 quarters = $\boxed{}$

2.   4 fifths = $\boxed{}$

3.   5 sixths = $\boxed{}$

4.   6 eighths = $\boxed{}$

5.   7 tenths = $\boxed{}$

Express each mixed number as an improper fraction.

> *Example*
>
> $1\dfrac{2}{3} = ?$
>
>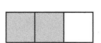
>
> 1 whole = $\boxed{3}$ thirds $\dfrac{2}{3} = \boxed{2}$ thirds
>
> There are $\boxed{5}$ thirds in $1\dfrac{2}{3}$.
>
> | An **improper fraction** is equal to or greater than 1. $\dfrac{5}{3}$ is an improper fraction. |
>
> $1\dfrac{2}{3} = \boxed{\dfrac{1}{3}} + \boxed{\dfrac{1}{3}} + \boxed{\dfrac{1}{3}} + \boxed{\dfrac{1}{3}} + \boxed{\dfrac{1}{3}} = \dfrac{5}{3}$
>
> So, $1\dfrac{2}{3} = \dfrac{5}{3}$.

6. $2\frac{1}{2}$

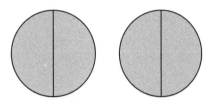

2 wholes = ☐ halves $\frac{1}{2}$ = ☐ half

There are ☐ halves in $2\frac{1}{2}$.

$2\frac{1}{2}$ = ☐ + ☐ + ☐ + ☐ + ☐ = ☐

7. $1\frac{3}{4}$

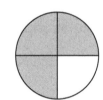

1 whole = ☐ quarters $\frac{3}{4}$ = ☐ quarters

There are ☐ quarters in $1\frac{3}{4}$.

$1\frac{3}{4}$ = ☐ + ☐ + ☐ + ☐ + ☐ + ☐ + ☐ = ☐

Express each mixed number as an improper fraction.
Use the models to help you.

Example

How many thirds are there in $2\frac{1}{3}$?

There are $\boxed{7}$ thirds in $2\frac{1}{3}$.

$2\frac{1}{3} = \boxed{7}$ thirds $= \boxed{\dfrac{7}{3}}$

---

8. How many sixths are there in $1\frac{5}{6}$?

There are $\boxed{}$ sixths in $1\frac{5}{6}$.

$1\frac{5}{6} = \boxed{}$ sixths $= \boxed{}$

9. How many eighths are there in $3\frac{5}{8}$?

There are $\boxed{}$ eighths in $3\frac{5}{8}$.

$3\frac{5}{8} = \boxed{}$ eighths $= \boxed{}$

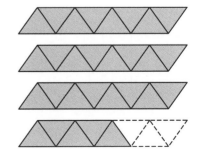

Express each improper fraction in simplest form.

Example

$$\frac{6}{4} = \text{?}$$

Method 1
Simplify the fractions shown by the shaded parts.

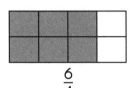

$$\frac{6}{4} \quad\quad\quad \frac{3}{2}$$

Method 2
Divide the numerator and the denominator by the same number.

So, $\frac{6}{4} = \boxed{\dfrac{3}{2}}$.

$$\frac{6}{4} \overset{\div 2}{\underset{\div 2}{=}} \frac{3}{2}$$

10. $\dfrac{12}{8} = \boxed{}$

11. $\dfrac{24}{15} = \boxed{}$

12. $\dfrac{30}{8} = \boxed{}$

13. $\dfrac{48}{36} = \boxed{}$

Write each fraction on the number line.

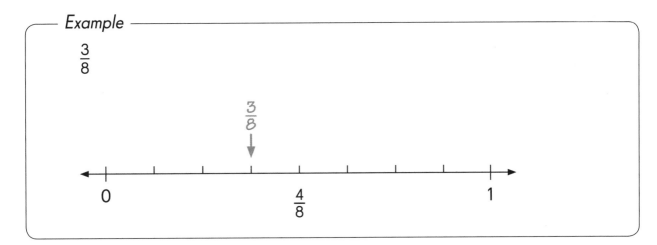

Example

$\frac{3}{8}$

$\overset{\frac{3}{8}}{\downarrow}$

0 ———————————————— $\frac{4}{8}$ ———————————————— 1

14. $\frac{3}{4}$ **15.** $\frac{7}{8}$ **16.** $\frac{1}{2}$

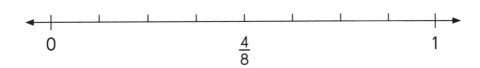

0 ———————————————— $\frac{4}{8}$ ———————————————— 1

$\frac{3}{4} = \frac{\boxed{}}{8}$

$\frac{1}{2} = \frac{\boxed{}}{8}$

Write the missing improper fraction in each box.

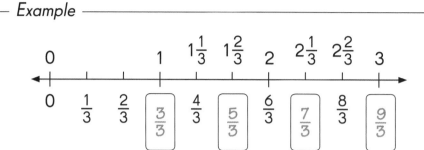

Example

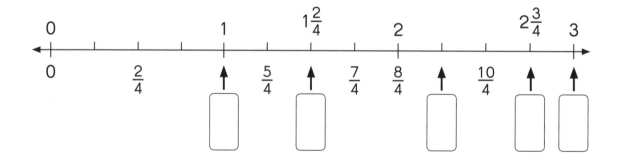

17.

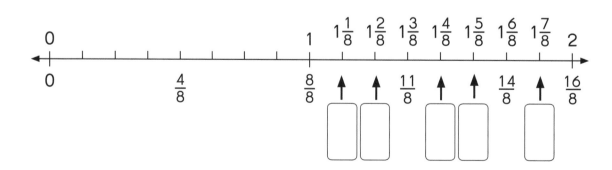

18.

Worksheet 5   Renaming Improper Fractions and Mixed Numbers

Complete each statement.

> *Example*
>
> 3 thirds is ____1____ whole.

1.

4 quarters is _____ whole.

2.

5 fifths is _____ whole.

3.

_____ sixths is 1 whole.

4.

_____ sevenths is 1 whole.

5.

_____ eighths is 1 whole.

Rename each improper fraction as a mixed number.
Use models to help you.

Example

$\frac{7}{3} = ?$

$\frac{7}{3} =$ [7] thirds

$=$ [6] thirds $+$ [1] third

$=$ [$\frac{6}{3}$] $+$ [$\frac{1}{3}$] $=$ [$2\frac{1}{3}$]

So, $\frac{7}{3} = 2\frac{1}{3}$.

6. $\frac{14}{5} =$ ☐ fifths

$=$ ☐ fifths $+$ ☐ fifths

$=$ ☐ $+$ ☐

$=$ ☐

7. $\frac{23}{6} =$ ☐ sixths

$=$ ☐ sixths $+$ ☐ sixths

$=$ ☐ $+$ ☐

$=$ ☐

Name: _____   **Date:** _____

Use the division rule to rename each improper fraction as a mixed number.

--- Example ---

$\dfrac{12}{5} = ?$

$$5\overline{)\;1\quad 2\;}$$

$\boxed{2}$

$1\quad 2$

$\boxed{1\quad 0}$

$\boxed{2}$

Division Rule:
Divide the numerator by the denominator.
$12 \div 5 = 2\,R\,2$

There are $\boxed{2}$ wholes and $\boxed{2}$ fifths in $\dfrac{12}{5}$.

So, $\dfrac{12}{5} = \underline{\quad 2\tfrac{2}{5} \quad}$.

---

8. $\dfrac{8}{3}$

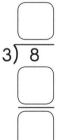

$$3\overline{)\;8\;}$$

There are $\boxed{}$ wholes and

$\boxed{}$ thirds in $\dfrac{8}{3}$.

So, $\dfrac{8}{3} = \underline{\qquad}$.

9. $\dfrac{37}{7}$

$$7\overline{)\;3\quad 7\;}$$

There are $\boxed{}$ wholes and

$\boxed{}$ sevenths in $\dfrac{37}{7}$.

So, $\dfrac{37}{7} = \underline{\qquad}$.

**Rename the improper fraction as a mixed number in simplest form.
Then check your answer using the division rule.**

Example

$\frac{45}{6} = ?$

$\frac{45}{6} = \boxed{45}$ sixths $= \boxed{42}$ sixths $+ \boxed{3}$ sixths

$= \boxed{\frac{42}{6}} + \boxed{\frac{3}{6}}$

$= \boxed{7} + \boxed{\frac{3}{6}}$

$= \boxed{7} + \boxed{\frac{1}{2}} = \boxed{7\frac{1}{2}}$

Check

$$\begin{array}{r} \boxed{7} \\ 6\overline{)45} \\ 42 \\ \hline \boxed{3} \end{array}$$

$45 \div 6 = \boxed{7}\ R\ \boxed{3}$

$\frac{45}{6} = \boxed{7\frac{3}{6}} = \boxed{7\frac{1}{2}}$

So, $\frac{45}{6} = 7\frac{1}{2}$.

---

10. $\frac{26}{4} = \boxed{}$ quarters $= \boxed{}$ quarters $+ \boxed{}$ quarters

$= \boxed{} + \boxed{}$

$= \boxed{} + \boxed{}$

$= \boxed{} + \boxed{} = \boxed{}$

Check

$$\begin{array}{r} \boxed{} \\ 4\overline{)26} \\ \boxed{} \\ \hline \boxed{} \end{array}$$

$26 \div 4 = \boxed{}\ R\ \boxed{}$

$\frac{26}{4} = \boxed{} = \boxed{}$

11. $\dfrac{48}{9} = \boxed{}$ ninths

$= \boxed{}$ ninths $+ \boxed{}$ ninths

$= \boxed{} + \boxed{}$

$= \boxed{} + \boxed{}$

$= \boxed{} + \boxed{}$

$= \boxed{}$

Check

$\boxed{}$

$9\overline{)4\ 8}$

$\dfrac{\boxed{}}{\boxed{}}$

$48 \div 9 = \boxed{} \text{ R } \boxed{}$

$\dfrac{48}{9} = \boxed{} = \boxed{}$

Use the multiplication rule to rename each mixed number as an improper fraction.

Example

$2\frac{1}{6} = ?$

$2\frac{1}{6} = 2 + \frac{1}{6}$

$\quad = \boxed{\dfrac{12}{6}} + \dfrac{1}{6} = \boxed{\dfrac{13}{6}}$

$\dfrac{2}{1} \;\overset{\times 6}{\underset{\times 6}{=}}\; \boxed{\dfrac{12}{6}}$ **Multiplication Rule**

So, $2\frac{1}{6} = \dfrac{13}{6}$.

---

12. $4\frac{1}{3} = 4 + \frac{1}{3}$

$\quad = \boxed{} + \dfrac{1}{3}$

$\quad = \boxed{}$

$\dfrac{4}{1} \;\overset{\times 3}{\underset{\times 3}{=}}\; \boxed{}$

13. $6\frac{2}{5} = 6 + \boxed{}$

$\quad = \boxed{} + \boxed{}$

$\quad = \boxed{}$

$\boxed{} \;\overset{\times \boxed{}}{\underset{\times \boxed{}}{=}}\; \boxed{}$

Rename each mixed number as an improper fraction in simplest form. Check your answer.

Example

$2\frac{3}{4} = ?$

$2\frac{3}{4} = 2 + \boxed{\dfrac{3}{4}}$

$= \boxed{\dfrac{8}{4}} + \boxed{\dfrac{3}{4}}$

$= \boxed{\dfrac{11}{4}}$

Check

Step 1   Multiply the whole number by the denominator.

$2 \times \boxed{4} = \boxed{8}$

Step 2   Add the product to the numerator.

$\boxed{8} + 3 = \boxed{11}$

There are $\boxed{11}$ quarters in $2\frac{3}{4}$.

So, $2\frac{3}{4} = \dfrac{11}{4}$.

14. $5\frac{1}{2} = 5 + \boxed{}$

$= \boxed{} + \boxed{}$

$= \boxed{}$

Check

$5 \times \boxed{} = \boxed{}$

$\boxed{} + \boxed{} = \boxed{}$

There are $\boxed{}$ halves in $5\frac{1}{2}$.

Name: _____   **Date:** _____

15. $7\dfrac{5}{6} =$ ☐ $+$ ☐

$=$ ☐ $+$ ☐

$=$ ☐

Check

$7 \times$ ◯ $=$ ◯

◯ $+$ ◯ $=$ ◯

There are ◯ sixths in $7\dfrac{5}{6}$.

16. $8\dfrac{8}{9} =$ ☐ $+$ ☐

$=$ ☐ $+$ ☐

$=$ ☐

Check

◯ $\times$ ◯ $=$ ◯

◯ $+$ ◯ $=$ ◯

There are ◯ ninths in $8\dfrac{8}{9}$.

© Marshall Cavendish International (Singapore) Private Limited.

Worksheet 6   Renaming Whole Numbers when Adding and Subtracting Fractions

Add. Express each answer as a mixed number in simplest form.

Example

$\frac{3}{4} + \frac{3}{4} = ?$

$\frac{3}{4} + \frac{3}{4} = \boxed{\dfrac{6}{4}}$

$= \boxed{\dfrac{4}{4}} + \boxed{\dfrac{2}{4}}$

$= \boxed{1} + \boxed{\dfrac{2}{4}}$

$= \boxed{1\dfrac{2}{4}}$

$= \boxed{1\dfrac{1}{2}}$

So, $\frac{3}{4} + \frac{3}{4} = 1\frac{1}{2}$.

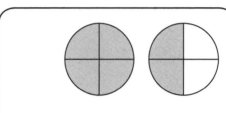

$\frac{6}{4} = \frac{4}{4} + \frac{2}{4}$

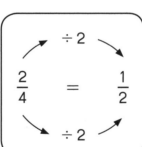

$\frac{2}{4} = \frac{1}{2}$ ÷ 2   ÷ 2

1. $\dfrac{4}{5} + \dfrac{3}{5} = \boxed{}$

$= \dfrac{5}{5} + \boxed{}$

$= 1 + \boxed{}$

$= \boxed{}$

2. $\dfrac{7}{12} + \dfrac{11}{12} = \boxed{}$

$= \boxed{} + \boxed{}$

$= \boxed{} + \boxed{}$

$= \boxed{}$

$= \boxed{}$

Find the equivalent fraction. Then add. Express each answer in simplest form.

Example

$\frac{2}{3} + \frac{7}{12} = ?$

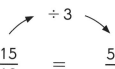

$\frac{2}{3} + \frac{7}{12} = \boxed{\frac{8}{12}} + \boxed{\frac{7}{12}}$

$\phantom{\frac{2}{3} + \frac{7}{12}} = \boxed{\frac{15}{12}}$

$\frac{15}{12} \quad\overset{\div 3}{=}\quad \frac{5}{4}$ ($\div 3$)

$\phantom{\frac{2}{3} + \frac{7}{12}} = \boxed{\frac{5}{4}} = \boxed{1\frac{1}{4}}$

So, $\frac{2}{3} + \frac{7}{12} = 1\frac{1}{4}$.

---

3. $\quad \frac{4}{5} + \frac{7}{10} = \boxed{} + \boxed{}$

$\phantom{\frac{4}{5} + \frac{7}{10}} = \boxed{}$

$\phantom{\frac{4}{5} + \frac{7}{10}} = \boxed{}$

$\phantom{\frac{4}{5} + \frac{7}{10}} = \boxed{}$

4. $\quad \frac{8}{9} + \frac{1}{3} = \boxed{} + \boxed{}$

$\phantom{\frac{8}{9} + \frac{1}{3}} = \boxed{}$

$\phantom{\frac{8}{9} + \frac{1}{3}} = \boxed{}$

Find the sum. Express each answer in simplest form.

> **Example**
>
> $\dfrac{2}{3} + \dfrac{5}{9} + \dfrac{4}{9} = ?$
>
> $\dfrac{2}{3} + \dfrac{5}{9} + \dfrac{4}{9} = \boxed{\dfrac{6}{9}} + \boxed{\dfrac{5}{9}} + \boxed{\dfrac{4}{9}}$
>
> $\qquad\qquad = \boxed{\dfrac{15}{9}}$
>
> $\qquad\qquad = \boxed{\dfrac{5}{3}} = \boxed{1\dfrac{2}{3}}$
>
> So, $\dfrac{2}{3} + \dfrac{5}{9} + \dfrac{4}{9} = 1\dfrac{2}{3}$.

5. $\dfrac{2}{3} + \dfrac{7}{12} + \dfrac{11}{12} = \boxed{} + \boxed{} + \boxed{}$

$\qquad\qquad\qquad = \boxed{}$

$\qquad\qquad\qquad = \boxed{}$

$\qquad\qquad\qquad = \boxed{}$

6. $1 + \dfrac{3}{4} + \dfrac{7}{12} = \boxed{} + \boxed{} + \boxed{}$

$= \boxed{}$

$= \boxed{}$

$= \boxed{}$

Express each whole number as a mixed number.

> **Example**
>
> $2 = \boxed{1}\,\dfrac{\boxed{3}}{3}$

7. $3 = 2\dfrac{\boxed{}}{8}$

8. $4 = \boxed{}\,\dfrac{\boxed{}}{12}$

9. $2 = 1\dfrac{5}{\boxed{}}$

10. $5 = \boxed{}\,\dfrac{4}{\boxed{}}$

Subtract each fraction from a whole number to get a mixed number.

--- Example ---

$2 - \frac{3}{4} = ?$

Method 1

$2 - \frac{3}{4} = \boxed{1\frac{4}{4}} - \boxed{\frac{3}{4}}$

$2 = 1 + 1$
$= 1 + \frac{4}{4} = 1\frac{4}{4}$

$= \boxed{1\frac{1}{4}}$

Method 2

$2 - \frac{3}{4} = \boxed{\frac{8}{4}} - \boxed{\frac{3}{4}}$

$2 = \frac{4}{4} + \frac{4}{4} = \frac{8}{4}$ or $2 = \frac{2}{1} = \frac{8}{4}$

$\times 4$ $\times 4$

$= \boxed{\frac{5}{4}}$

$= \boxed{1\frac{1}{4}}$

So, $2 - \frac{3}{4} = 1\frac{1}{4}$.

11. $1 - \frac{3}{8} = \boxed{} - \boxed{}$

$= \boxed{}$

12. $3 - \frac{5}{12} = \boxed{} - \boxed{}$

$= \boxed{}$

13. $3 - \dfrac{5}{9} =$ ☐ $-$ ☐

$=$ ☐

$=$ ☐

14. $4 - \dfrac{2}{3} =$ ☐ $-$ ☐

$=$ ☐

$=$ ☐

Subtract. Express your answer in simplest form.

Example

$\dfrac{2}{3} - \dfrac{5}{9} = \, ?$

$\dfrac{2}{3} - \dfrac{5}{9} = \boxed{\dfrac{6}{9}} - \boxed{\dfrac{5}{9}}$

$\phantom{\dfrac{2}{3} - \dfrac{5}{9}} = \boxed{\dfrac{1}{9}}$

So, $\dfrac{2}{3} - \dfrac{5}{9} = \dfrac{1}{9}$.

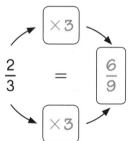

$\dfrac{2}{3} \quad \xrightarrow{\times 3} \quad = \quad \dfrac{6}{9} \quad \xleftarrow{\times 3}$

15. $\dfrac{3}{4} - \dfrac{7}{12} = \boxed{} - \boxed{}$

$= \boxed{}$

$= \boxed{}$

$\dfrac{3}{4} \overset{\times 3}{\underset{\times 3}{=}} \boxed{}$

16. $\dfrac{5}{6} - \dfrac{5}{12} = \boxed{} - \boxed{}$

$= \boxed{}$

$\dfrac{5}{6} \overset{\times 2}{\underset{\times \boxed{}}{=}} \boxed{}$

17. $\dfrac{4}{5} - \dfrac{3}{10} = \boxed{} - \boxed{}$

$= \boxed{}$

$= \boxed{}$

$\dfrac{4}{5} \overset{\times \boxed{}}{\underset{\times \boxed{}}{=}} \boxed{}$

Worksheet 7   Fraction of a Set

Find the fraction of each set.

Example

$\frac{1}{3}$ of 12 = ?

12 pretzels are divided into 3 equal groups.

$\frac{1}{3}$ of 12 means 1 of the 3 groups of pretzels.

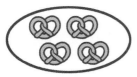 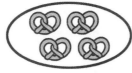 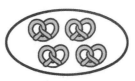

3 groups of pretzels → 12 pretzels
1 group of pretzels → 4 pretzels

So, $\frac{1}{3}$ of 12 is _____4_____.

---

1. $\frac{1}{4}$ of 8 = ☐

2. $\frac{2}{3}$ of 24 = ☐

3. $\frac{3}{4}$ of 28 = ☐

4. $\frac{5}{9}$ of 27 = ☐

5. $\frac{3}{8}$ of 48 = ☐

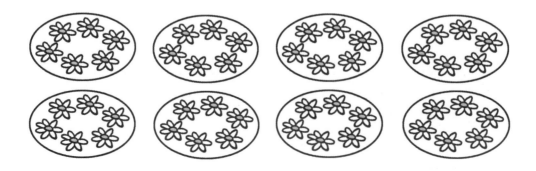

Answer the questions.

> *Example*
>
> How many toys are shaded?
>
> _____9_____ toys are shaded.

6. 24 toys are divided into equal groups.

There are _____ groups of toys, and _____ groups are shaded.

7. What fraction of the set of toys are shaded?

The shaded parts = $\dfrac{\Box}{\Box}$ of the set.

8. Write the missing numbers on the model.

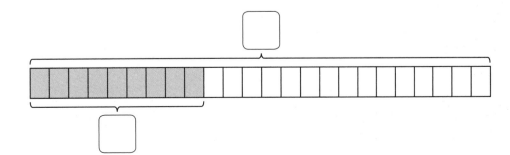

Name: _____ **Date:** _____

Write the missing numbers.

> ── *Example* ──────────────────────────────────
>
> 15 fruits are divided into ____3____ groups.

9. There are _____ fruits in each group.

10. _____ out of the 15 fruits in the set are shaded.

11. Color the parts of the model to show the number of fruits that are shaded.

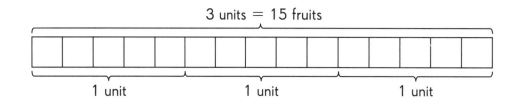

3 units = 15 fruits

1 unit   1 unit   1 unit

12. What fraction of the fruits are shaded?

The shaded parts = $\dfrac{\square}{\square}$ of the set.

13. From the model, 1 unit ⟶ _____ fruits

2 units ⟶ _____ fruits

Find the fractional part of each number. Use models to help you.

Example

$\frac{2}{3}$ of 12 = ?

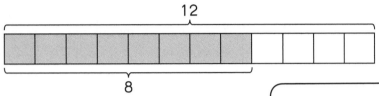

12

8

_____3_____ units = _____12_____

1 unit = _____4_____

2 units = _____4_____ × _____2_____ = _____8_____

So, $\frac{2}{3}$ of 12 is _____8_____.

Divide 12 into 3 equal parts.
The shaded parts = $\frac{2}{3}$ of the set.

14. $\frac{3}{8}$ of 32

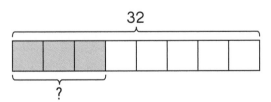

32

?

_____ units = _____

1 unit = _____ ÷ _____ = _____

3 units = _____ × _____ = _____

So, $\frac{3}{8}$ of 32 = _____.

Find the fractional part of each number. Show your work.

Example

$\frac{3}{5}$ of 35 = ?

$\frac{3}{5} \times 35 = \dfrac{\boxed{3} \times \boxed{35}}{5}$

$= \dfrac{\boxed{105}}{5}$

$= \boxed{21}$

The word "of" means to multiply.

So, $\frac{3}{5}$ of 35 = 21.

15. $\frac{3}{4}$ of 28

$\frac{3}{4} \times 28 = \dfrac{\boxed{} \times \boxed{}}{4}$

$= \dfrac{\boxed{}}{4}$

$= \boxed{}$

16. $\frac{2}{7}$ of 56

$\frac{2}{7} \times 56 = \dfrac{\boxed{} \times \boxed{}}{\boxed{}}$

$= \dfrac{\boxed{}}{\boxed{}}$

$= \boxed{}$

17. $\frac{3}{8}$ of 64

18. $\frac{7}{11}$ of 44

Worksheet 8   Real-World Problems: Fractions

Solve. Show your work.

> *Example*
>
> Three friends shared a pie. Susan ate $\frac{1}{4}$ of the pie.
>
> Daniel ate $\frac{3}{8}$ of the pie. Joe ate $\frac{1}{8}$ of the pie.
>
> What fraction of the pie did they eat altogether?
>
> $\frac{1}{4} + \frac{3}{8} + \frac{1}{8} = \boxed{\frac{2}{8}} + \frac{3}{8} + \frac{1}{8}$
>
> $\qquad\qquad = \boxed{\frac{6}{8}} = \boxed{\frac{3}{4}}$
>
>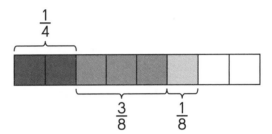
>
> They ate ___$\frac{3}{4}$___ of the pie.

1. Lisa, Sam, and Marco each bought some dried fruit.

   Lisa bought $\frac{2}{3}$ pound of dried fruit. Sam and Marco each bought $\frac{5}{6}$ pound

   of dried fruit. How much dried fruit did they buy altogether?

   $\frac{2}{3} + \frac{5}{6} + \frac{5}{6} = \boxed{} + \frac{5}{6} + \frac{5}{6}$

   $\qquad\qquad = \boxed{} = \boxed{} = \boxed{}$

   They bought _____ pounds of dried fruit altogether.

2. Mrs. Jackson baked muffins one day. She used $\frac{1}{4}$ kilogram of flour to bake the first batch of muffins. She used $\frac{7}{12}$ kilogram of flour to bake the second batch, and another $\frac{11}{12}$ kilogram of flour for the third batch. How much flour did she use altogether?

$$\frac{1}{4} + \frac{7}{12} + \frac{11}{12} = \boxed{} + \frac{7}{12} + \frac{11}{12}$$

$$= \boxed{} = \boxed{}$$

She used _____ kilograms of flour altogether.

3. Edison made a fruit salad. He mixed $\frac{7}{12}$ pound of apples and $\frac{3}{4}$ pound of strawberries. He then added $\frac{5}{12}$ pound of banana. What was the total weight of the fruit salad?

─ *Example* ───

Kathy has 1 loaf of whole grain bread.

She cuts $\frac{2}{3}$ of it for her friend and $\frac{1}{12}$ for herself.

What fraction of the bread is left?

Method 1

$1 - \frac{2}{3} - \frac{1}{12}$

$= \frac{12}{12} - \frac{8}{12} - \frac{1}{12}$

$= \frac{3}{12}$

$= \frac{1}{4}$

____$\frac{1}{4}$____ loaf of bread is left.

Method 2

$\frac{2}{3} + \frac{1}{12} = \frac{8}{12} + \frac{1}{12}$

$= \frac{9}{12}$

$\frac{12}{12} - \frac{9}{12} = \frac{3}{12}$

$= \frac{1}{4}$

____$\frac{1}{4}$____ loaf of bread is left.

4. Sam spent $\frac{1}{3}$ of his time playing soccer and $\frac{4}{9}$ of his time doing homework. He spent the rest of his time playing computer games. How much of his time did Sam spend playing computer games?

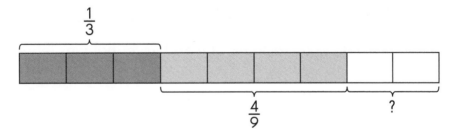

$\frac{1}{3} + \frac{4}{9} = \frac{\boxed{}}{9} + \frac{4}{9} = \frac{\boxed{}}{9}$

$1 - \boxed{} = \frac{9}{9} - \boxed{} = \boxed{}$

Sam spent _____ of his time playing computer games.

5. Latoya bought a pizza. She ate $\frac{1}{6}$ of the pizza and gave $\frac{1}{3}$ of it to her sister. She kept the rest of the pizza for her grandmother. How much of the pizza did Latoya keep for her grandmother?

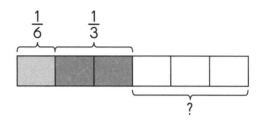

$$\frac{1}{6} + \frac{1}{3} = \boxed{} + \boxed{} = \boxed{}$$

$$1 - \boxed{} = \boxed{} - \boxed{} = \boxed{} = \boxed{}$$

Latoya kept _____ of the pizza for her grandmother.

6. Pam made mixed juice from carrot juice and apple juice. She filled a jug with $\frac{7}{8}$ liter of carrot juice and $\frac{3}{4}$ liter of apple juice. Pam then drank $\frac{3}{8}$ liter of the mixed juice. Find the amount of mixed juice that was left in the jug.

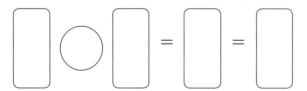

_____ liters of mixed juice was left in the jug.

Example

Ling bought a total of 12 apples. Of the apples she bought, 8 are red apples and 4 are green apples.

a. What fraction of the apples are red?

b. What fraction of the apples are green?

a. 8 out of 12 is $\dfrac{\boxed{8}}{\boxed{12}}$.

$\dfrac{8}{12} = \dfrac{\boxed{2}}{\boxed{3}}$ $\underline{\ \ \frac{2}{3}\ \ }$ of the apples are red.

b. $1 - \underline{\ \ \frac{2}{3}\ \ } = \underline{\ \ \frac{1}{3}\ \ }$

$\underline{\ \ \frac{1}{3}\ \ }$ of the apples are green.

---

7. Elan has a bag of 10 marbles. He gives 4 marbles to his brother.

a. What fraction of his marbles does Elan give away?

4 out of 10 is $\dfrac{\boxed{}}{\boxed{}}$.

Elan gives away _____ of his marbles.

b. What fraction of the marbles are left?

$1 - \underline{\hspace{2cm}} = \underline{\hspace{2cm}}$

_____ of the marbles are left.

8. Bernice has a ribbon that is 12 centimeters long. She cuts 8 centimeters off the length of the ribbon. What fraction of the ribbon is left?

Example

Dianne has $72. She uses $\frac{5}{9}$ of it to buy a present for her father.

How much money does Dianne have left?

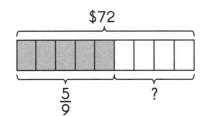

$72

$\frac{5}{9}$?

Method 1

9 units = $72

1 unit = $72 ÷ 9

= $8

4 units = $8 × 4

= $32

Dianne has ___$32___ left.

Method 2

$\frac{5}{9}$ of $72 = $\frac{5}{9}$ × $72

= $\frac{\$360}{9}$

= $40

Dianne spent $40.

$72 − $40 = $32

Dianne has ___$32___ left.

9. Winton was given $14 to spend at his school fair. He spent $\frac{3}{7}$ of the money playing games. How much money did Winton have left?

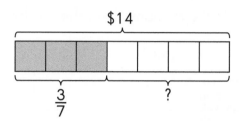

$14

$\frac{3}{7}$?

Method 1

_____ units = $_____

1 unit = $_____

_____ units = $_____ × _____

= $_____

$14 − $_____ = $_____

Winton had $_____ left.

Method 2

$\frac{3}{7}$ of $14 = _____ × $_____

= _____ × $_____

= $_____

He spent $_____.

$14 − $_____ = $_____

Winton had $_____ left.

10. Chris planted carrots on $\frac{5}{9}$ of his farm and tulips on the rest of the land. The total area of his farm is 621 square meters.

Find the area of the land on which he planted tulips.

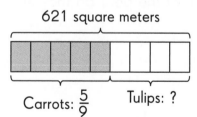

621 square meters

Carrots: $\frac{5}{9}$ Tulips: ?

Method 1

Method 2

11. Of all the seats in an airplane, $\frac{1}{3}$ are business-class seats, and the rest are economy-class seats.

There are 156 seats in the airplane. Find the number of economy-class seats.

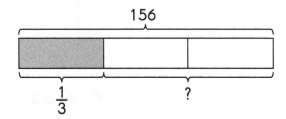

Method 1   **Method 2**

12. Sally cuts a pear into 8 equal pieces. She gives each of her 6 students one piece each. What fraction of the pear do they eat altogether?

13. Mr. Lee has 12 visitors. He prepares 12 glasses of orange juice for his visitors. Each glass contains $\frac{2}{9}$ liters of orange juice. How many liters of orange juice has Mr. Lee prepared altogether?

Worksheet 9   Line Plots with Fractions of a Unit

Solve.

1. Jeff went to a garden and collected some leaves. He measured the lengths
    of the leaves and recorded them as follows:
    3 cm, 5 cm, 8 cm, 4 cm, 3 cm, 4 cm, 7 cm, 6 cm, 3 cm, 3 cm, 2 cm, 4 cm,
    5 cm, 5 cm, 6 cm, 7 cm, 6 cm, 5 cm, 4 cm, 5 cm, 4 cm, 5 cm, 1 cm.

    Draw a table and record the data.

Length of Leaves	Tally	Number of Leaves

    From the table draw a graph below. Use an ✗ to represent one leaf.

2. The graph shows the mode of transportation of children to school daily.

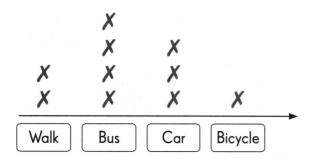

a. Which is the most common way children go to school?

b. Why do you think so?

c. Which is the least common way children go to school?

d. Why do you think so?

e. How many more children go to school by bus than by bicycle?

Answers

Chapter 1

Worksheet 1

1. 95,530
2. 28,614
3. 70,451
4. 68,973
5. twenty-seven thousand, four hundred ninety-five
6. forty-eight thousand, two hundred thirty
7. eighty-four thousand
8. ninety thousand, six hundred five
9. 52,800
10. 83,640
11. 29,351
12. 60,284
13. 36,516
14. 70,014
15. 80,000 90,000 100,000
16. 19,030 19,040 19,050
17. 30,700 30,800 30,900
18. 70,800 80,900 91,000
19. 7, 2, 8, 4, 5
20. 2, 4, 3, 1, 9
21. 3, 5, 0
22. 9, 1, 6
23. tens
24. hundreds
25. thousands
26. ten thousands
27. 90
28. 90,000
29. 900
30. 9
31. 98,653
32. 78,423
33. ten thousands
34. 8
35. thousands, 6,000
36. 10
37. $42,859 = 40,000 + \underline{2,000} + 800 + \underline{50} + 9$
38. $61,734 = \underline{60,000} + 1,000 + \underline{700} + 30 + \underline{4}$
39. $24,570 = \underline{20,000} + \underline{4,000} + \underline{500} + \underline{70}$
40. $68,037 = \underline{60,000} + \underline{8,000} + \underline{0} + \underline{30} + \underline{7}$
41. 84,796 85,796
    Rule: Add 1,000.
42. 34,400 24,400
    Rule: Subtract 10,000.
43. 35,180 34,175
    Rule: Subtract 1,005.

Worksheet 2

− 5,000; + 5,000

1. 75,000
2. 65,000
3. 45,000
4. 35,000
5. >
6. <
7. 37,482 52,104 58,369
8. 79,780
9. 4,000
10. 95,325
11. 40,400
12. 52,700 47,700
    Rule: Subtract 5,000.
13. 58,578 64,778
    Rule: Add 3,100.
14. 17,440 17,080
    Rule: Subtract 120.

Worksheet 3

1. a. 12; 1; 2   b. 13; 1; 3; 13
   c. 14; 1; 4; 14   d. 15; 1; 5; 15
2. a. 11; 1; 1   b. 16; 1; 6; 160
   c. 11; 1; 1; 110   d. 12; 1; 2; 120
3. a. 12; 1; 2   b. 14; 1; 4; 1,400
   c. 11; 1; 1; 1,100 d. 10; 1; 0; 1,000
4. a. 4,979   b. 8,799
   c. 7,988   d. 9,889
5. a. 7,690   b. 5,835
   c. 8,527   d. 8,163
6. a. 5; 5   b. 5; 5
7. a. 4; 4   b. 8; 8   c. 5; 5   d. 7; 7
8. a. 2; 2; 3; 23
   b. 4; 8; 4; 2; 42
   c. 3; 6; 3; 4; 340
   d. 1; 10; 5; 1; 5; 1,500
   e. 5; 10; 7; 5; 3; 530
   f. 6; 10; 9; 6; 1; 6,100
9. a. 4,531   b. 1,222
   c. 777   d. 785
   e. 3,525   f. 1,313
   g. 26,666   h. 35,655
   i. 15,315   j. 16,208

Chapter 2

Worksheet 1

1. 742; 500; 200; 700; 700; Yes
2. 349; 800; 500; 300; 300; Yes
3. 7,181; 5,000; 2,000; 7,000; Yes
4. 5,621; 15,000; 9,000; 6,000; Yes
5. $3,000 + 1,000 = 4,000$

6. $9,000 - 2,000 = 7,000$

7. $333; 700 - 400 = 300; 333$ is close to 300, so the answer is reasonable.

8. $5,965; 2,000 + 3,000 = 5,000; 5,965$ is close to 5,000, so the answer is reasonable.

9. $2,731; 5,000 - 2,000 = 3,000; 2,731$ is close to 3,000, so the answer is reasonable.

10. $978; 326; 300 \times 3 = 900$; Yes

11. $534; 267; 300 \times 2 = 600$; Yes

12. $216; 50 \times 4 = 200; 216$ is close to 200, so the answer is reasonable.

13. $336; 100 \times 3 = 300; 336$ is close to 300, so the answer is reasonable.

14. $496 \div 4 = \underline{124}$
    $4 \times \underline{120} = \underline{480}$
    $4 \times \underline{130} = \underline{520}$
    $\underline{480} \div 4 = \underline{120}$
    The answer is <u>reasonable</u>.

15. $516 \div 2 = \underline{258}$
    $2 \times \underline{250} = \underline{500}$
    $2 \times \underline{260} = \underline{520}$
    $\underline{520} \div \underline{2} = \underline{260}$
    The answer is <u>reasonable</u>.

16. $780 \div 5 = \underline{156}$
    $\underline{5} \times \underline{150} = \underline{750}$
    $\underline{5} \times \underline{160} = \underline{800}$
    $\underline{800} \div \underline{5} = \underline{160}$
    The answer is <u>reasonable</u>.

17. An exact answer is needed.
    $\$111 - \$52 - \$33 - \$21 = \$5$ left
    Ms. Katy has enough money to buy all these things. She will have $5 left.

18. An exact answer is needed.
    $784 \text{ mL} - 309 \text{ mL} = 475 \text{ mL}$
    They drink 475 milliliters of milk in the afternoon.

19. An estimate is needed.
    $14.99 is about $15.
    5.29×2 is about $\$5 \times 2 = \$10$.
    $8.99 is about $9.
    $\$15 + \$10 + \$9 = \$34$
    Caithlin spent about $34 in all.

Worksheet 2
1. $105; 105, 5$
2. $105; 105, 35, 3$
3. $96; 96, 8, 12, 96$
4. $104; 104; 26, 4, 104$
5. $2 \text{ R } 4$; No; No
6. 3; Yes; Yes

7. 4; Yes; Yes

8. $24 = 1 \times \underline{24}$
    $= 2 \times \underline{12}$
    $= \underline{3} \times \underline{8}$
    $= \underline{4} \times 6$
    The factors of 24 are $\underline{1}, \underline{2}, \underline{3}, \underline{4}, \underline{6}, \underline{8}$, $\underline{12}$, and $\underline{24}$.

9. $54 = \underline{1} \times \underline{54}$
    $= \underline{2} \times \underline{27}$
    $= \underline{3} \times \underline{18}$
    $= \underline{6} \times \underline{9}$
    The factors of 54 are $\underline{1}, \underline{2}, \underline{3}, \underline{6}, \underline{9}, \underline{18}$, $\underline{27}$, and $\underline{54}$.

10. $72 = \underline{1} \times \underline{72}$
    $= \underline{2} \times \underline{36}$
    $= \underline{3} \times \underline{24}$
    $= \underline{4} \times \underline{18}$
    $= \underline{6} \times \underline{12}$
    $= \underline{8} \times 9$
    The factors of 72 are $\underline{1}, \underline{2}, \underline{3}, \underline{4}, \underline{6}, \underline{8}, \underline{9}$, $\underline{12}, \underline{18}, \underline{24}, \underline{36}$, and $\underline{72}$.

11. $108 = \underline{1} \times \underline{108}$
    $= \underline{2} \times \underline{54}$
    $= \underline{3} \times \underline{36}$
    $= \underline{4} \times \underline{27}$
    $= \underline{6} \times \underline{18}$
    $= \underline{9} \times \underline{12}$
    The factors of 108 are $\underline{1}, \underline{2}, \underline{3}, \underline{4}, \underline{6}, \underline{9}$, $\underline{12}, \underline{18}, \underline{27}, \underline{36}, \underline{54}, \underline{108}$.

12. $16; 17 \text{ R } 1$; No   13. $14; 19$; Yes

14. $5 \text{ R } 5; 12$; No

15. 21: ①, 3, ⑦, 21
    28: ①, 2, 4, ⑦, 14, 28
    The greatest common factor is $\underline{7}$.

16. 32: ①, ②, 4, 8, 16, 32
    42: ①, ②, 3, 6, 7, 14, 21, 42
    The greatest common factor is $\underline{2}$.

17. 48: ①, ②, ③, ④, ⑥, ⑧, ⑫, 16, ㉔, 48
    72: ①, ②, ③, ④, ⑥, ⑧, 9, ⑫, 18, ㉔, 36, 72
    The greatest common factor is $\underline{24}$.

18.
```
2 | 12, 24
2 |  6, 12
3 |  3,  6
        1,  2
```
    $\underline{2} \times \underline{2} \times \underline{3} = \underline{12}$
    The greatest common factor is $\underline{12}$.

19.
```
2 | 36, 42
3 | 18, 21
     6,  7
```
$2 \times 3 = 6$

The greatest common factor is 6.

20.
```
2 | 54, 72
3 | 27, 36
3 |  9, 12
     3,  4
```
$2 \times 3 \times 3 = 18$

The greatest common factor is 18.

21.
```
3 | 15, 42
     5, 14
```
The greatest common factor is 3.

22. 15, 24, 36, 54, and 75

23. 10, 15 and 75

24. 15 and 75

25. $5 = 1 \times 5$
The factors of 5 are 1 and 5.
So, 5 is a prime number.

26. $9 = 1 \times 9$
$= 3 \times 3$
The factors of 9 are 1, 3, and 9.
So, 9 is not a prime number.

27. $11 = 1 \times 11$
The factors of 11 are 1 and 11.
So, 11 is a prime number.

28. $26 = 1 \times 26$
$= 2 \times 13$
The factors of 26 are 1, 2, 13, and 26.
So, 26 is not a prime number.

29. $20 = 1 \times 20$
$= 2 \times 10$
$= 4 \times 5$
The factors of 20 are 1, 2, 4, 5, 10, and 20.
So, 20 is a composite number.

30. $13 = 1 \times 13$
The factors of 13 are 1 and 13.
So, 13 is not a composite number.

31. $63 = 1 \times 63$
$= 3 \times 21$
$= 7 \times 9$
The factors of 63 are 1, 3, 7, 9, 21, and 63.
So, 63 is a composite number.

32. $41 = 1 \times 41$
The factors of 41 are 1 and 41.
So, 41 is not a composite number.

33. 13, 41

34. A prime number has only 2 different factors.
13 has only 2 different factors, 1 and 13.
So, 13 is a prime number. 41 has only 2 different factors, 1 and 41. So, 41 is a prime number.

Worksheet 3

1. 6; 12; 18; 24; 30; 36; 42; 48
6, 12, 18, 24, 30, 36, 42, and 48

2. 8; 16; 24; 32; 40; 48; 56; 64
8, 16, 24, 32, 40, 48, 56, and 64

3. 23

4. 51

5. 17, 27

6. 39, 47, 49, 79

7.
```
     8
 3)2 4
   2 4
     0
```
✔ Yes, 24 is the eighth multiple of 3.

8.
```
     7
 6)4 5
   4 2
     3
```
✔ No, 45 is not a multiple of 6. It cannot be divided exactly by 6.

9.
```
   1 2
 8)9 6
   8 0
   1 6
   1 6
     0
```
✔ Yes, 96 is the twelfth multiple of 8.

10. 35; 35

11. 24, 48; 24

12. 2: 2, 4, 6, 8, (10), 12, 14, 16, 18, (20)
5: 5, (10), 15, (20)
The least common multiple is 10.

13. 6: 6, 12, (18), 24, 30, (36)
9: 9, (18), 27, (36), 42
The least common multiple is 18.

14.
```
3 | 9, 18
3 | 3,  6
    1,  2
```
$3 \times 3 \times 1 \times 2 = 18$

15. 2 | 14, 28
    7 | 7, 14
        1, 2

    2 × 7 × 1 × 2 = 28

16. 3 | 15, 45
    5 | 5, 15
        1, 3

    3 × 5 × 1 × 3 = 45

17. 2 | 12, 52
    2 | 6, 26
        3, 13

    2 × 2 × 3 × 13 = 156

Worksheet 4

1. a. 14 × 3   b. 13 × 5   c. 12 × 7

2. a.

   b.

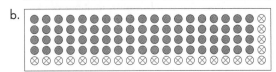

3. a. 13; 8; 10; 8; 3; 80; 24; 104
   b. 18; 9; 10; 9; 8; 90; 72; 162

4. a. 10; 70; 4; 28; 70; 28; 98
   b. 5; 50; 5; 40; 50; 40; 90
   c. 10; 20; 2; 12; 20; 12; 32
   d. 6; 60; 5; 30; 60; 30; 90

5. a. 6; 10; 6; 3; 60; 18; 78
   b. 4; 20; 4; 3; 80; 12; 92
   c. 5; 30; 5; 7; 150; 35; 185

6. a. 126 b. 216 c. 210 d. 235 e. 232

Chapter 3

Worksheet 1

1. 8   2. 2, 8

3. 48, 4, 8   4. 20, 2

5. 42, 4, 2   6. 18, 1, 8

7. 28, 2, 8   8. 48, 4, 8

9. 40, 4

10. 6; 9; 18, 8; 16; 16,896

         1
      5, 6 3 2
  ×   3
    1 6, 8 9 6

11. 5; 5; 5, 9; 4; 25; 25, 4, 29,095

      4   4
    5, 8 1 9
  ×   5
  2 9, 0 9 5

12. 0; 8; 28, 2, 8; 32; 32, 2, 34; 34,880

      2
    8, 7 2 0
  ×   4
  3 4, 8 8 0

13. 54, 5, 4; 0; 0, 5, 5; 30, 3; 36; 36, 3, 39;
    39,054

      3   5
    6, 5 0 9
  ×   6
  3 9, 0 5 4

14. 56, 5, 6; 42; 42, 5, 47, 4, 7; 49; 49, 53, 5,
    3; 28; 28, 5, 33; 33,376

      5 4 5
    4, 7 6 8
  ×   7
  3 3, 3 7 6

15.   1
    7, 6 4 3
  ×   2
  1 5, 2 8 6

16.   7 1 2
    6, 9 2 3
  ×   8
  5 5, 3 8 4

17.   5, 3 4 7
  ×   3
       2 1 → 7 × 3 = 21
     1 2 0 → 40 × 3 = 120
     9 0 0 → 300 × 3 = 900
  1 5, 0 0 0 → 5,000 × 3 = 15,000
  1 6, 0 4 1

18.   4, 8 3 5
  ×   7
       3 5 → 5 × 7 = 35
     2 1 0 → 30 × 7 = 210
    5, 6 0 0 → 800 × 7 = 5,600
  2 8, 0 0 0 → 4,000 × 7 = 28,000
  3 3, 8 4 5

19.   7 0 0
  ×   8
  5, 6 0 0

20.   1 3
    9 2 8
  ×   4
  3, 7 1 2

21.   2 1
   4, 7 2 6
  ×   3
  1 4, 1 7 8

22.   1
   9, 2 1 0
  ×   6
  5 5, 2 6 0

Worksheet 2

1. 12
2. 230
3. 8
4. 600
5. 21
6. 1,500
7. 8; 48; 480
8. 3; 48; 480
9. 105; 1,050
10. 204; 2,040
11. 25; 2,500
12. 3, 33; 3,300
13. 7, 10; 42; 420
14. 74, 9, 10; 666, 10; 6,660
15. 42, 2; 4,200, 2; 8,400
16. 973, 100; 2,919, 100; 291,900

17.
```
      9 2
  ×   4 3
  ¹2 7 6
  3, 6 8 0
  3, 9 5 6
```

18.
```
      ³⁴3 6
  ×     5 7
      2 5 2
  ¹1, 8 0 0
  2, 0 5 2
```

19.
```
  ¹₁
    2 4 0
  ×   3 3
    7 2 0
  7, 2 0 0
  7, 9 2 0
```

20.
```
      ⁴
      ⁷
    5 0 8
  ×   6 9
  ¹4,¹5 7 2
  3 0, 4 8 0
  3 5, 0 5 2
```

21.
```
      9 0 0
  ×     8 1
      9 0 0
  7 2, 0 0 0
  7 2, 9 0 0
```

22.
```
    ² ⁴
    ¹ ³
    6 3 7
  ×   7 5
  3,¹1 8 5
  4 4, 5 9 0
  4 7, 7 7 5
```

23. 70 × 50 = 3,500
    68 × 52 is about 3,500.

24. 40 × 70 = 2,800
    42 × 73 is about 2,800.

25. 200 × 80 = 16,000
    239 × 77 is about 16,000.

26. 1,000 × 40 = 40,000
    984 × 36 is about 40,000.

27. 1,566; 60 × 30 = 1,800
    1,566 is close to 1,800, so the answer is reasonable.
```
    ¹
    ⁵5 8
  ×   2 7
    4 0 6
  1, 1 6 0
  1, 5 6 6
```

28. 4,725; 60 × 80 = 4,800
    4,725 is close to 4,800, so the answer is reasonable.
```
    ²
    ¹6 3
  ×   7 5
    3 1 5
  4, 4 1 0
  4, 7 2 5
```

29. 4,658; 140 × 30 = 4,200; reasonable
```
    ¹ ²
    ¹ ²
    1 3 7
  ×   3 4
    5 4 8
  4, 1 1 0
  4, 6 5 8
```

30. 63,080; 800 × 80 = 64,000; reasonable
```
    ⁴
    ¹
    7 6 0
  ×   8 3
  ¹2, 2 8 0
  6 0, 8 0 0
  6 3, 0 8 0
```

31. 79,734; 800 × 100 = 80,000; reasonable
```
    ¹ ¹
    ¹ ¹
    8 2 2
  ×   9 7
  ¹5,¹7 5 4
  7 3, 9 8 0
  7 9, 7 3 4
```

32. 38,315; 500 × 80 = 40,000; reasonable
```
    ⁵ ³
    ⁷ ⁴
    4 8 5
  ×   7 9
  ¹4,¹3 6 5
  3 3, 9 5 0
  3 8, 3 1 5
```

Worksheet 3

1. 8, 1, 3; 3, 30; 30, 6
```
      1 1 6
  5)5 8 0
    5 0 0
      8 0
      5 0
      3 0
      3 0
        0
```

2. 2, 1; 1, 10; 10, 16, 16, 4; 2

```
      2 4 2
  4) 9 6 8
      8 0 0
      1 6 8
      1 6 0
          8
          8
          0
```

3.
```
      1                1                1 4
  6) 8 5 8    →    6) 8 5 8    →    6) 8 5 8
      6 0 0            6 0 0            6 0 0
          2            2 5 8            2 5 8
                                        2 4 0
                                            1
```

```
      1 4 3              1 4
  6) 8 5 8    ←      6) 8 5 8    ←
      6 0 0              6 0 0
      2 5 8              2 5 8
      2 4 0              2 4 0
          1 8                1 8
          1 8
            0
```

10.
```
      1 6 4
  6) 9 8 4
      6 0 0
      3 8 4
      3 6 0
          2 4
          2 4
            0
```

11.
```
      1 6 8
  4) 6 7 2
      4 0 0
      2 7 2
      2 4 0
          3 2
          3 2
            0
```

Worksheet 4

1.
```
       1, 1 7 3
  4) 4, 6 9 2
      4, 0 0 0
          6 9 2
          4 0 0
          2 9 2
          2 8 0
            1 2
            1 2
              0
```

2.
```
           8 1 4
  9) 7, 3 2 6
      7, 2 0 0
            1 2 6
              9 0
              3 6
              3 6
                0
```

3.
```
           6 3 1 R 8
  9) 5, 6 8 7
      5, 4 0 0
            2 8 7
            2 7 0
              1 7
                 9
                 8
```

4.
```
       1, 3 4 2 R 1
  7) 9, 3 9 5
      7, 0 0 0
      2, 3 9 5
      2, 1 0 0
            2 9 5
            2 8 0
              1 5
              1 4
                 1
```

5. 110 × 6 = 660   120 × 6 = 720

680 is closer to 660 than to 720.

So, 680 ÷ 6 is about 660 ÷ 6 = 110.

6. 800 × 8 = 6,400   900 × 8 = 7,200

6,882 is closer to 7,200 than to 6,400.

So, 6,882 ÷ 8 is about 7,200 ÷ 8 = 900.

4.
```
        8 5
  9) 7 6 5
      7 2 0
          4 5
          4 5
            0
```

5.
```
        5 9
  8) 4 7 2
      4 0 0
          7 2
          7 2
            0
```

6.
```
        1 2 9
  7) 9 0 3
      7 0 0
      2 0 3
      1 4 0
          6 3
          6 3
            0
```

7.
```
        1 3 9
  5) 6 9 5
      5 0 0
      1 9 5
      1 5 0
          4 5
          4 5
            0
```

8.
```
        2 8 9
  2) 5 7 8
      4 0 0
      1 7 8
      1 6 0
          1 8
          1 8
            0
```

9.
```
        2 8 9
  3) 8 6 7
      6 0 0
      2 6 7
      2 4 0
          2 7
          2 7
            0
```

8. 7,500, 1,500; 1,500, reasonable

$$
\begin{array}{r}
1,473 \text{ R } 4 \\
5{\overline{\smash{\big)}\,7,369}} \\
\underline{5,000} \\
2,369 \\
\underline{2,000} \\
369 \\
\underline{350} \\
19 \\
\underline{15} \\
4
\end{array}
$$

9. 6,400, 800; 800, reasonable

$$
\begin{array}{r}
843 \text{ R } 6 \\
8{\overline{\smash{\big)}\,6,750}} \\
\underline{6,400} \\
350 \\
\underline{320} \\
30 \\
\underline{24} \\
6
\end{array}
$$

Worksheet 5

1. $\underline{298} + \underline{509} = \underline{807}$

   $807 \times 21 = \underline{16,947}$

   They pack $\underline{16,947}$ boxes of pears in 21 days.

2.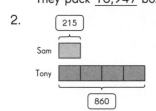

   a. 1 unit ⟶ $\underline{215}$

   4 units ⟶ $\underline{215} \times 4 = \underline{860}$

   Tony has $\underline{860}$ marbles.

   b. $\underline{860} \div 9 = \underline{95}$ R $\underline{5}$

   He has $\underline{95}$ full boxes.

   c. $\underline{5}$ marbles are not packed in a full box.

3.
   Boys
   Girls ⎬ 118
   106 12

   a. Number of girls
   = 106 + 12 = 118
   Number of boys and girls
   = 106 + 118 = 224
   There are $\underline{224}$ students in the school.

b. $224 \div 8 = 28$
   There are $\underline{28}$ students in each class.

4.
   1 computer
   2 mobile phones ⎬ $782 + $418

   a. $782 + $418 = $1,200
   The total cost of all the items is $\underline{\$1,200}$.

   b. 4 units ⟶ $1,200
   2 units ⟶ $1,200 \div 2 = $600
   The computer costs $\underline{\$600}$.

5.
   1 table
   5 chairs ⎬ $2,750 − $262

   a. $2,750 − $262 = $2,488
   The total cost is $\underline{\$2,488}$.

   b. 8 units ⟶ $2,488
   1 unit ⟶ $2,488 \div 8 = $311
   The cost of each chair is $311.
   $311 \times 5 = $1,555
   The 5 chairs cost $\underline{\$1,555}$.

Chapter 4

Worksheet 1

1. $2,374 - 1,470 = \underline{904}$

2. $4,000 - 1,720 = \underline{2,280}$

3. a

4. //   5. /

6. ⅬⱧⱦ ////   7. ///

8.

Type of Pet	Dog	Cat	Hamster	Fish	Others
Number	5	2	1	9	3

9. 7 groups of 5 = 35
   $35 + 1 = \underline{36}$

10. cows

11. $36 - 12 = \underline{24}$

12. $18 + 3 + 36 + 12 = \underline{69}$

13.

Sport	Tally	Number of Students
Basketball	///	3
Volleyball	//	2
Cycling	//	2
Soccer	/	1

14.

Number Shown	One	Two	Three	Four	Five	Six
Number of times tossed	4	3	2	3	4	3

4 + 3 + 2 + 3 + 4 + 3 = 19
The number cube was tossed <u>19</u> times.

15.

Country	USA	France	Kenya	Singapore	Russia
Number of Participants	12	20	15	8	5

12 + 20 + 15 + 8 + 5 = 60

16.

Favorite Fruit	Tally	Number of Students
apple	LHT ///	8
pear	LHT //	7
orange	LHT	5
apricot	////	4
plum	//	2

17. January   18. May
19. 8 cm − 5 cm = <u>3 cm</u>
20. April, June
21. 8 + 6 + 5 + 3 + 2 + 3 = <u>27 cm</u>
22. February
23.

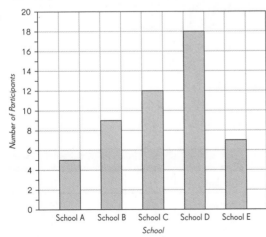

24. dolls
25. 24 − 6 = 18
    <u>18</u> more dolls than monkeys were sold.

26. 14 − 8 = 6
    <u>6</u> fewer airplanes than dolphins were sold.
27. 24 − 18 = 6
    <u>6</u> more cars must be sold to equal the number of dolls sold.
28. 14 + 6 + 18 + 24 + 8 = 70
    A total of <u>70</u> toys were sold during the month of March.

Worksheet 2
1. W77, P88, Q10   2. T48, S27, P88
3. T48   4. <u>S27</u> or <u>Y32</u>
5. guavas   6. 34 − 15 = <u>19</u>
7. 14 − 9 = <u>5</u>   8. apples
9. 20 + 8 + 9 + 21 + 4 = <u>62</u>
10. 200 − 173 = <u>27</u>
11.

Mode of Transportation	Bus	Taxi	Walk	Cycle
Number of Students	76	1	54	42

12. Taxi
13. 76 + 42 = <u>118</u>   14. 54 − 42 = <u>12</u>

Day	Number of Green Apples	Number of Red Apples	Total Number of Apples
Monday	60	20	80
Tuesday	15	50	65
Wednesday	30	70	100
Thursday	50	70	120
Friday	40	195	235
Total	195	405	600

15. Friday   16. Tuesday
17. Red apples   18. Monday
19. 235 − 65 = <u>170</u>

Worksheet 3
1. 450 cents = <u>$4.50</u>
2. 375 ÷ 75 = 5
   Jerry buys <u>5</u> mangoes.
3. 1,000
4. 4,000 − 1,000 = <u>3,000</u> liters
5. a. Friday, Saturday
   b. 4,000 − 2,000 = <u>2,000</u> liters

6. 5,000 − 1,000 = 4,000 liters
    The family uses 4,000 liters of water from
    Monday through Sunday.
    4,000 ÷ 4 = 1,000 liters
    Each family member uses 1,000 liters of water.

7. 40 grams   8.   50 grams
9. 15 centimeters   10. 30 centimeters

Chapter 5

Worksheet 1

1. 48 + 26 + 32 + 57 + 97 = 260 mL
    260 ÷ 5 = 52 mL
    The average volume of the containers is
    52 millimeters.

2. Total distance = 536 + 450 + 152 + 824 +
                      375 + 459 = 2,796 km
    Average distance = 2,796 ÷ 6 = 466 km
    The average distance traveled is 466 kilometers.

3. Total volume of milk
    = 375 × 8 = 3,000 mL
    The total volume of milk is 3,000 milliliters.

4. $28 × 185 = $5,180
    She spent $5,180.

5. Total distance Mary walked in 5 days
    = 750 × 5 = 3,750 m
    She walked 3,750 meters in 5 days.

6. 7 × 68 = 476 cm
    The total length of their arms is 476 centimeters.

7. a. 79 × 4 = 316
       The total score for the four tests is 316.
    b. 67 + 74 + 92 = 233
       316 − 233 = 83
       Joe's score for the third test is 83.

8. Washington

9. 10 + 9 + 13 + 11 + 15 = 58 games

10. 58 ÷ 2 = 29 games

11. $8 + $7 + $3 = $18
    He paid $18 altogether.

12. $18 ÷ 3 = $6
    The average price of a kilogram of nuts is $6.

Worksheet 2

1. a. 802   b. 802
2. 90   3.   60
4. a. 111, 113

b. Mean $= \dfrac{111 + 113}{2} = \dfrac{224}{2} = 112$ m
   The median is 112 meters.

5. 74 cm, 86 cm, 98 cm, 102 cm, 110 cm, 124 cm
    Mean $= \dfrac{98 + 102}{2} = \dfrac{200}{2} = 100$ cm
    The median height is 100 centimeters.

6. a. 1   b. 1   c. 20

7. a.

```
                X   X
                X   X
                X   X   X
        X       X   X   X   X
    X   X   X   X   X   X   X   X
    X   X   X   X   X   X   X   X
   ──┼───┼───┼───┼───┼───┼───┼──
     3   4   5   6   7   8   9
         Number of Leaves
```

    b. 4   c. 5, 6

8. a. 7 kg   b. 12 kg
    c. The range of mass lifted
       = 12 kg − 7 kg
       = 5 kg

9. 2 ribbons have a length of 12 cm → 2 × 12
                                         = 24 cm
    4 ribbons have a length of 20 cm → 4 × 20
                                         = 80 cm
    2 ribbons have a length of 28 cm → 2 × 28
                                         = 56 cm
    Total length of all the ribbons = 24 + 80 + 56
                                      = 160 cm
    Mean $= \dfrac{160}{8} = 20$ cm
    The mean length of the ribbons is 20 centimeters.

10.

```
        X
        X
        X           X
        X           X   X
    X   X           X   X
    X   X           X   X
    X   X   X       X   X
    X   X   X       X   X
    X   X   X   X   X   X
    X   X   X   X   X   X
   ──┼───┼───┼───┼───┼──
     5   6   7   8   9
       Number of Marbles
```

    6 bags has 5 marbles each   → 6 × 5 = 30
    10 bags have 6 marbles each → 10 × 6 = 60
    4 bags have 7 marbles each → 4 × 7 = 28
    8 bags have 8 marbles each → 8 × 8 = 64
    7 bags have 9 marbles each → 7 × 9 = 63
    Total number of marbles
    = 30 + 60 + 28 + 64 + 63 = 245
    Mean $= \dfrac{245}{35} = 7$
    The mean number of marbles is 7.

11. $7 - 2 = 5$

The range of the number of people living in the houses is 5.

12. 3   13. 1

14. Total number of people
$= 3 \times 2 + 5 \times 3 + 5 \times 4 + 4 \times 5 + 2 \times 6 + 1 \times 7 = 80$

Total number of houses
$= 3 + 5 + 5 + 4 + 2 + 1 = 20$

Mean $= \dfrac{80}{20} = 4$

The mean of the number of people living in each house is 4.

15. The modes are 3 and 4.

Worksheet 3

1. 42   2. 3

3. 24, 27, 34, 41, 45, 47, 48, 52, 58, 63

4.

Number of Rolls	
Stem	**Leaves**
2	4 7
3	4
4	1 5 7 8
5	2 8
6	3

5. a. 1   b. 24
c. 63   d. 10

6. a. 46, 53, 58
b. Range = <u>96</u> lb − 32 lb = <u>64</u> lb
c. 96 pounds

7. a. 42   b. 34   c. 65   d. 21
e. $65 - 21 = 44$ cm
The range of the lengths is <u>44</u> centimeters.

f. Median $= \dfrac{42 + 44}{2} = 43$ cm
The median length of the snakes is <u>43</u> centimeters.

8. a.

Amount of Money	
Stem	**Leaves**
4	2 6
5	9
6	0 4 5 8
7	5 9

b. There is no mode as all the amounts appear the same number of times.

c. Range = <u>$79</u> − <u>$42</u> = <u>$37</u>
The range of the amount of money collected is <u>$37</u>.

d. The middle number is 64. So, the median amount of money collected is <u>$64</u>.

e. $42 + $46 + $59 + $60 + $64 + $65 + $68 + $75 + $79 = $558
A total of <u>$558</u> was collected.

f. $\dfrac{\$558}{9} = \$62$

The average amount of money collected by each stall is <u>$62</u>.

Worksheet 4

1. more likely   2. equally likely

3. a. more likely   b. less likely

4. a. certain   b. impossible

5. yellow or green; equally likely

6. green or yellow; less likely

7. green; impossible

8. a   9. b   10. a

11.   12.   13.

Worksheet 5

1. Odd numbers: 1, 3, 5
Number of favorable outcomes = 3
Probability of landing on an odd number
$= \dfrac{3}{6} = \dfrac{1}{2}$
The probability of landing on an odd number is $\dfrac{1}{2}$.

2. Numbers less than 5: 1, 2, 3, 4
Number of favorable outcomes = 4
Number of possible outcomes = 6
Probability of landing on a number less than
$5 = \dfrac{4}{6} = \dfrac{2}{3}$
The probability of landing on a number less than 5 is $\dfrac{2}{3}$.

3. Number more than 3: 4, 5, 6
Number of favorable outcomes = 3
Number of possible outcomes = 6
Probability of landing on a number greater than $3 = \dfrac{3}{6} = \dfrac{1}{2}$

The probability of landing on a number greater than 3 is $\frac{1}{2}$.

4. $\frac{5}{10} = \frac{1}{2}$; equally likely   5. $\frac{2}{10} = \frac{1}{5}$; less likely

6. $\frac{7}{10}$; more likely   7. $\frac{0}{10} = 0$; impossible

8. $\frac{2}{10} = \frac{1}{5}$; less likely   9. $\frac{7}{10}$; more likely

10. $\frac{5}{10} = \frac{1}{2}$; equally likely 11. $\frac{10}{10} = 1$; certain

12. $\frac{0}{10} = 0$; impossible

Worksheet 6

1. Total income of 4 workers
   $= 4 \times \underline{\$1{,}250} = \underline{\$5{,}000}$
   Income of 3 workers = $3,420
   Income of the 4th worker
   $= \underline{\$5{,}000} - \underline{\$3{,}420} = \underline{\$1{,}580}$
   The income of the 4th worker is $\underline{\$1{,}580}$.

2. Cost of 3 toys = $3 \times \underline{\$40} = \underline{\$120}$
   Cost of 5 toys = $5 \times \underline{\$50} = \underline{\$250}$
   Cost of 8 toys = $\underline{\$120} + \underline{\$250} = \underline{\$370}$
   Cost of the remaining 2 toys
   $= \underline{\$780} - \underline{\$370} = \underline{\$410}$
   Mean cost of the 2 toys $= \dfrac{\boxed{\$410}}{2} = \underline{\$205}$

   The mean cost of the remaining 2 toys is $\underline{\$205}$.

3. Total mass of the goat and sheep
   $= 2 \times \underline{78 \text{ kg}} = \underline{156 \text{ kg}}$
   2 units → Total mass $- \underline{6 \text{ kg}}$
   $\underline{156 \text{ kg}} - \underline{6 \text{ kg}} = \underline{150 \text{ kg}}$
   1 unit → $\dfrac{\boxed{150}}{2} = \underline{75 \text{ kg}}$
   The mass of the goat is $\underline{75}$ kilograms.
   $\underline{75 \text{ kg}} + \underline{6 \text{ kg}} = \underline{81 \text{ kg}}$
   The mass of the sheep is $\underline{81}$ kilograms.

4. a. Number of roses delivered to 5 florists
      $= \underline{108} + \underline{156} + \underline{96} + \underline{120} + \underline{84} = \underline{564}$
      Number of roses delivered to Florist F
      $= $ Total number of roses $- \underline{564}$
      $= \underline{684} - \underline{564} = \underline{120}$
      The number of roses he delivered to Florist F is $\underline{120}$.
   b. Range $= \underline{156} - \underline{84} = \underline{72}$
      The range of the number of roses delivered is $\underline{72}$.
   c. 120

---

d. The numbers ordered from least to greatest:
   $\underline{84}$, $\underline{96}$, $\underline{108}$, $\underline{120}$, $\underline{120}$, $\underline{156}$
   The middle numbers are $\underline{108}$ and $\underline{120}$.
   Mean $= \dfrac{108 + 120}{2} = \underline{114}$
   The median of the set of data is $\underline{114}$.

5. a. Longest distance $= \underline{8 \text{ m}} + \underline{66 \text{ m}} = \underline{74 \text{ m}}$
      The longest distance the javelin was thrown is $\underline{74}$ meters.
   b. Total distance $= \underline{70 \text{ m}} \times 5 = \underline{350 \text{ m}}$
      The missing data
      $= \underline{350 \text{ m}} - 68 \text{ m} - 72 \text{ m} - 66 \text{ m} - \underline{74 \text{ m}}$
      $= \underline{70 \text{ m}}$
      The missing data is $\underline{70}$ meters.
   c. The distances ordered from least to greatest:
      $66, 68, \underline{70}, 72, 74$
      The median distance is $\underline{70}$ meters.

6. a. Total amount $-$ Amount of money deposited in 11 months
      $= \$960 - \$63 - \$66 - \$68 - \$72 -$
      $\$80 - \$84 - \$84 - \$89 - \$91 -$
      $\$92 - \$97$
      $= \underline{\$74}$
      The missing data in stem 7 is $\underline{\$74}$.
   b. $84
   c. Mean $= \dfrac{\$80 + \$84}{2} = \$82$
      The median of the set of data is $\underline{\$82}$.
   d. $\$97 - \$63 = \underline{\$34}$

7. a. 6   b. 6
   c. $1 \times 3 \text{ lb} = 3 \text{ lb}$
      $2 \times 4 \text{ lb} = 8 \text{ lb}$
      $3 \times 5 \text{ lb} = 15 \text{ lb}$
      $5 \times 6 \text{ lb} = 30 \text{ lb}$
      $4 \times 7 \text{ lb} = 28 \text{ lb}$
      $3 \times 8 \text{ lb} = 24 \text{ lb}$
      $2 \times 9 \text{ lb} = 18 \text{ lb}$
      Total weight $= 3 + 8 + 15 + 30 + 28 +$
      $24 + 18 = 126 \text{ lb}$
      Total cost $= \$3 \times 126 = \$378$
      The total cost of all the watermelons is $\underline{\$378}$.

8. a. i. less likely   ii. less likely
      iii. more likely   iv. certain
   b. i. Number of favorable outcomes $= \underline{6}$
      Number of possible outcomes
      $= 16 + 1 + 3 = \underline{20}$
      Probability of drawing a red marble
      $= \dfrac{6}{20} = \dfrac{3}{10}$

The probability that a red marble is drawn is $\frac{3}{10}$.

ii. Number of favorable outcomes = <u>18</u>
Number of possible outcomes = <u>20</u>
Probability of drawing a red, blue, or green marble = $\frac{18}{20} = \frac{9}{10}$
The probability that Tyron draws a red, blue, or green marble is $\frac{9}{10}$.

Chapter 6

Worksheet 1

1. $\frac{4}{8}$

2. $\frac{9}{15}$

3. $\frac{3}{4}$

4. $\times 5; \frac{35}{45}$

5. $\frac{4}{6}; \times 4$

6. $\times 6; \times 6$

7. $\frac{1}{4} = \boxed{\frac{2}{8}}$

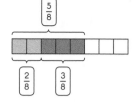

$\frac{3}{8} + \frac{1}{4} = \frac{3}{8} + \boxed{\frac{2}{8}} = \boxed{\frac{5}{8}}$

8. $\frac{1}{3} = \boxed{\frac{4}{12}}$

$\frac{1}{12} + \frac{1}{3} = \boxed{\frac{1}{12}} + \boxed{\frac{4}{12}} = \boxed{\frac{5}{12}}$

9. $\frac{1}{2} = \boxed{\frac{4}{8}}$

$\frac{1}{2} = \frac{4}{8}$ ($\times 4$)

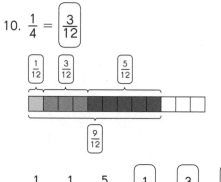

$\frac{1}{8} + \frac{1}{2} + \frac{3}{8} = \frac{1}{8} + \boxed{\frac{4}{8}} + \frac{3}{8}$

$= \boxed{\frac{8}{8}} = \boxed{1}$

10. $\frac{1}{4} = \boxed{\frac{3}{12}}$

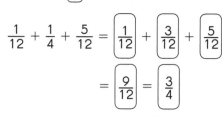

$\frac{1}{12} + \frac{1}{4} + \frac{5}{12} = \boxed{\frac{1}{12}} + \boxed{\frac{3}{12}} + \boxed{\frac{5}{12}}$

$= \boxed{\frac{9}{12}} = \boxed{\frac{3}{4}}$

11. $\frac{6}{17}$ 12. $\frac{3}{7}$

13. $\frac{1}{3}$ 14. $\frac{5}{7}$

15. $\frac{6}{9} = \frac{2}{3}$ 16. $\frac{12}{12} = 1$

17. $\frac{3}{10} + \frac{2}{5} + \frac{1}{10} = \frac{3}{10} + \boxed{\frac{4}{10}} + \frac{1}{10}$

$= \boxed{\frac{8}{10}} = \boxed{\frac{4}{5}}$

$\frac{2}{5} = \frac{4}{10}$ ($\times 2$)

18. $\frac{1}{4} + \frac{1}{6} + \frac{5}{12}$

$= \boxed{\frac{3}{12}} + \boxed{\frac{2}{12}} + \frac{5}{12}$

$= \boxed{\frac{10}{12}} = \boxed{\frac{5}{6}}$

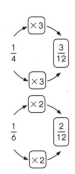

9. $\frac{7}{12} - \frac{1}{4} = \frac{7}{12} - \frac{3}{12}$

$= \frac{4}{12} = \frac{1}{3}$

10. $\frac{11}{12} - \frac{1}{6} = \frac{11}{12} - \frac{2}{12}$

$= \frac{9}{12} = \frac{3}{4}$

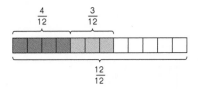

Worksheet 2

1. $\frac{6}{8}$

2. $\frac{4}{10}$

3. $\frac{2}{8} = \frac{1}{4}$

4. $\frac{2}{10} = \frac{1}{5}$

5. $\frac{3}{12} = \frac{1}{4}$

6. $\frac{3}{4} = \boxed{\frac{9}{12}}$

$\frac{11}{12} - \frac{3}{4} = \frac{11}{12} - \boxed{\frac{9}{12}} = \boxed{\frac{2}{12}} = \boxed{\frac{1}{6}}$

7. $1 = \boxed{\frac{9}{9}}$

$1 - \frac{5}{9} = \boxed{\frac{9}{9}} - \frac{5}{9} = \boxed{\frac{4}{9}}$

8. $1 - \frac{7}{10} = \boxed{\frac{10}{10}} - \frac{7}{10} = \frac{3}{10}$

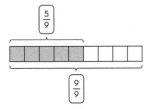

11. $1 - \frac{4}{12} - \frac{1}{4} = \boxed{\frac{12}{12}} - \frac{4}{12} - \boxed{\frac{3}{12}}$

$= \boxed{\frac{5}{12}}$

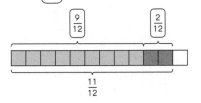

12. $1 - \frac{2}{10} - \frac{3}{5} = \boxed{\frac{10}{10}} - \boxed{\frac{2}{10}} - \boxed{\frac{6}{10}}$

$= \boxed{\frac{2}{10}} = \boxed{\frac{1}{5}}$

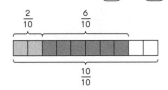

13. $\frac{17}{21} - \frac{2}{3} = \frac{17}{21} - \boxed{\frac{14}{21}}$

$= \boxed{\frac{3}{21}} = \boxed{\frac{1}{7}}$

14. $1 - \frac{1}{4} - \frac{5}{12} = \boxed{\frac{12}{12}} - \boxed{\frac{3}{12}} - \frac{5}{12}$

$= \boxed{\frac{4}{12}} = \boxed{\frac{1}{3}}$

15. $1 - \frac{1}{4} - \frac{3}{20} = \boxed{\frac{20}{20}} - \boxed{\frac{5}{20}} - \frac{3}{20}$

$= \boxed{\frac{12}{20}} = \boxed{\frac{3}{5}}$

Worksheet 3

1. $\boxed{1} + \boxed{\dfrac{3}{8}} = 1\dfrac{3}{8}$ 2. $\boxed{2} + \boxed{\dfrac{3}{5}} = 2\dfrac{3}{5}$

3. $\boxed{3} + \boxed{\dfrac{3}{5}} = 3\dfrac{3}{5}$ 4. $\boxed{2} + \boxed{\dfrac{7}{12}} = 2\dfrac{7}{12}$

Exercises 5, 6 and 7:

$$1\tfrac{1}{3} \qquad 2\tfrac{2}{3} \qquad 3\tfrac{2}{3}$$

(number line from 0 to 4)

8. $2\dfrac{1}{4}$ 9. $3\dfrac{3}{4}$

10. $1 + \boxed{\dfrac{6}{8}} = \boxed{1\dfrac{6}{8}} = 1\dfrac{3}{4}$

11. $\boxed{2} + \boxed{\dfrac{8}{14}} = \boxed{2\dfrac{8}{14}} = \boxed{2\dfrac{4}{7}}$

Worksheet 4

1. $\dfrac{3}{4}$ 2. $\dfrac{4}{5}$

3. $\dfrac{5}{6}$ 4. $\dfrac{6}{8}$

5. $\dfrac{7}{10}$

6. 4; 1; 5;
$$2\dfrac{1}{2} = \dfrac{1}{2} + \dfrac{1}{2} + \dfrac{1}{2} + \dfrac{1}{2} + \dfrac{1}{2} = \dfrac{5}{2}$$

7. 4; 3; 7;
$$1\dfrac{3}{4} = \dfrac{1}{4} + \dfrac{1}{4} + \dfrac{1}{4} + \dfrac{1}{4} + \dfrac{1}{4} + \dfrac{1}{4} + \dfrac{1}{4} = \dfrac{7}{4}$$

8. 11; 11; $\dfrac{11}{6}$ 9. 29; 29; $\dfrac{29}{8}$

10. $\dfrac{3}{2}$ 11. $\dfrac{8}{5}$

12. $\dfrac{15}{4}$ 13. $\dfrac{4}{3}$

Exercises 14, 15 and 16:

$$\tfrac{1}{2} \quad \tfrac{3}{4} \ \tfrac{7}{8}$$

(number line from 0 to 1, with $\tfrac{4}{8}$ marked)

17. $\dfrac{4}{4}; \dfrac{6}{4}; \dfrac{9}{4}; \dfrac{11}{4}; \dfrac{12}{4}$ 18. $\dfrac{9}{8}; \dfrac{10}{8}; \dfrac{12}{8}; \dfrac{13}{8}; \dfrac{15}{8}$

Worksheet 5

1. 1   2. 1
3. 6   4. 7
5. 8

6. $\dfrac{14}{5} = \boxed{14}$ fifths $= \boxed{10}$ fifths $+ \boxed{4}$ fifths
$$= \dfrac{10}{5} + \dfrac{4}{5} = 2\dfrac{4}{5}$$

7. $\dfrac{23}{6} = \boxed{23}$ sixths $= \boxed{18}$ sixths $+ \boxed{5}$ sixths
$$= \dfrac{18}{6} + \dfrac{5}{6} = 3\dfrac{5}{6}$$

8. 2; 2
$$3)\overline{8} \quad \dfrac{2}{} \\ \dfrac{6}{2}$$
$\dfrac{8}{3} = 2\dfrac{2}{3}$

9. 5; 2
$$7)\overline{3\ 7} \quad \dfrac{5}{} \\ \dfrac{3\ 5}{2}$$
$\dfrac{37}{7} = 5\dfrac{2}{7}$

10. $\dfrac{26}{4} = \boxed{26}$ quarters
$= \boxed{24}$ quarters $+ \boxed{2}$ quarters
$= \boxed{\dfrac{24}{4}} + \boxed{\dfrac{2}{4}}$

Check
$4)\overline{2\ 6}$, $\dfrac{2\ 4}{2}$ $26 \div 4 = 6$ R 2

$\dfrac{26}{4} = 6\dfrac{2}{4} = 6\dfrac{1}{2}$

$= \boxed{6} + \boxed{\dfrac{2}{4}}$

$= \boxed{6} + \boxed{\dfrac{1}{2}} = \boxed{6\dfrac{1}{2}}$

11. $\dfrac{48}{9} = \boxed{48}$ ninths
$= \boxed{45}$ ninths $+ \boxed{3}$ ninths
$= \boxed{\dfrac{45}{9}} + \boxed{\dfrac{3}{9}}$

Check
$9)\overline{4\ 8}$, $\dfrac{4\ 5}{3}$ $48 \div 9 = 5$ R 3

$\dfrac{48}{9} = 5\dfrac{3}{9} = 5\dfrac{1}{3}$

$= \boxed{5} + \boxed{\dfrac{3}{9}}$

$= \boxed{5} + \boxed{\dfrac{1}{3}} = 5\dfrac{1}{3}$

12. $4\dfrac{1}{3} = 4 + \dfrac{1}{3} = \boxed{\dfrac{12}{3}} + \dfrac{1}{3} = \boxed{\dfrac{13}{3}}$

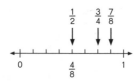

$\dfrac{4}{1} = \dfrac{12}{3}$ ($\times 3$)

13. $6\frac{2}{5} = 6 + \boxed{\frac{2}{5}}$

$\quad = \boxed{\frac{30}{5}} + \boxed{\frac{2}{5}} = \boxed{\frac{32}{5}}$

$\boxed{\frac{6}{1}} = \boxed{\frac{30}{5}}$ (×5)

14. $5\frac{1}{2} = 5 + \boxed{\frac{1}{2}}$

Check
$5 \times \boxed{2} = \boxed{10}$
$\boxed{10} + \boxed{1} = \boxed{11}$
There are $\boxed{11}$ halves in $5\frac{1}{2}$.

$\quad = \boxed{\frac{10}{2}} + \boxed{\frac{1}{2}}$

$\quad = \boxed{\frac{11}{2}}$

15. $7\frac{5}{6} = \boxed{7} + \boxed{\frac{5}{6}}$

Check
$7 \times \boxed{6} = \boxed{42}$
$\boxed{42} + \boxed{5} = \boxed{47}$
There are $\boxed{47}$ sixths in $7\frac{5}{6}$.

$\quad = \boxed{\frac{42}{6}} + \boxed{\frac{5}{6}}$

$\quad = \boxed{\frac{47}{6}}$

16. $8\frac{8}{9} = \boxed{8} + \boxed{\frac{8}{9}}$

Check
$\boxed{8} \times \boxed{9} = \boxed{72}$
$\boxed{72} + \boxed{8} = \boxed{80}$
There are $\boxed{80}$ ninths in $8\frac{8}{9}$.

$\quad = \boxed{\frac{72}{9}} + \boxed{\frac{8}{9}}$

$\quad = \boxed{\frac{80}{9}}$

Worksheet 6

1. $\frac{4}{5} + \frac{3}{5} = \boxed{\frac{7}{5}} = \frac{5}{5} + \boxed{\frac{2}{5}} = 1 + \boxed{\frac{2}{5}}$

$\quad = \boxed{1\frac{2}{5}}$

2. $\frac{7}{12} + \frac{11}{12} = \boxed{\frac{18}{12}} = \boxed{\frac{12}{12}} + \boxed{\frac{6}{12}}$

$\quad = \boxed{1} + \boxed{\frac{6}{12}}$

$\quad = \boxed{1\frac{6}{12}} = \boxed{1\frac{1}{2}}$

3. $\frac{4}{5} + \frac{7}{10} = \boxed{\frac{8}{10}} + \boxed{\frac{7}{10}} = \boxed{\frac{15}{10}} = \boxed{\frac{3}{2}} = \boxed{1\frac{1}{2}}$

4. $\frac{8}{9} + \frac{1}{3} = \boxed{\frac{8}{9}} + \boxed{\frac{3}{9}} = \boxed{\frac{11}{9}} = \boxed{1\frac{2}{9}}$

5. $\frac{2}{3} + \frac{7}{12} + \frac{11}{12} = \boxed{\frac{8}{12}} + \boxed{\frac{7}{12}} + \boxed{\frac{11}{12}}$

$\quad = \boxed{\frac{26}{12}} = \boxed{\frac{13}{6}} = \boxed{2\frac{1}{6}}$

6. $1 + \frac{3}{4} + \frac{7}{12} = \boxed{\frac{12}{12}} + \boxed{\frac{9}{12}} + \boxed{\frac{7}{12}}$

$\quad = \boxed{\frac{28}{12}} = \boxed{\frac{7}{3}} = \boxed{2\frac{1}{3}}$

7. $3 = 2\dfrac{\boxed{8}}{\boxed{8}}$

8. $4 = \boxed{3}\dfrac{\boxed{12}}{\boxed{12}}$

9. $2 = 1\dfrac{\boxed{5}}{\boxed{5}}$

10. $5 = \boxed{4}\dfrac{4}{\boxed{4}}$

11. $1 - \frac{3}{8} = \boxed{\frac{8}{8}} - \boxed{\frac{3}{8}} = \boxed{\frac{5}{8}}$

12. $3 - \frac{5}{12} = \boxed{2\frac{12}{12}} - \boxed{\frac{5}{12}} = \boxed{2\frac{7}{12}}$

13. $3 - \frac{5}{9} = \boxed{\frac{27}{9}} - \boxed{\frac{5}{9}} = \boxed{\frac{22}{9}} = \boxed{2\frac{4}{9}}$

14. $4 - \frac{2}{3} = \boxed{\frac{12}{3}} - \boxed{\frac{2}{3}} = \boxed{\frac{10}{3}} = \boxed{3\frac{1}{3}}$

15. $\frac{3}{4} - \frac{7}{12} = \frac{9}{12} - \frac{7}{12} = \frac{2}{12} = \frac{1}{6}$

$\frac{3}{4} = \boxed{\frac{9}{12}}$ (×3)

16. $\frac{5}{6} - \frac{5}{12} = \frac{10}{12} - \frac{5}{12} = \frac{5}{12}$

$\frac{5}{6} = \boxed{\frac{10}{12}}$ (×2)

17. $\frac{4}{5} - \frac{3}{10} = \frac{8}{10} - \frac{3}{10} = \frac{5}{10} = \frac{1}{2}$

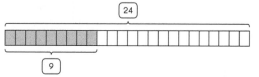

Worksheet 7

1. 2
2. 16
3. 21
4. 15
5. 18
6. 8; 3
7. $\frac{3}{8}$

8.

| 24 |
|
| 9 |

9. 5
10. 10

11.

3 units = 15 fruits

1 unit   1 unit   1 unit

12. $\frac{10}{15}$ or $\frac{2}{3}$
13. 5; 10

14. $\underline{8}$ units $= \underline{32}$

   1 unit $= \underline{32} \div \underline{8} = \underline{4}$

   3 units $= \underline{4} \times \underline{3} = \underline{12}$

   So, $\frac{3}{8}$ of 32 $= \underline{12}$.

15. 3; 28; 84; 21
16. 2; 56; 7; 112; 7; 16
17. 24
18. 28

Worksheet 8

1. $\frac{2}{3} + \frac{5}{6} + \frac{5}{6} = \boxed{\frac{4}{6}} + \frac{5}{6} + \frac{5}{6}$

   $= \boxed{\frac{14}{6}} = \boxed{\frac{7}{3}} = \boxed{2\frac{1}{3}}$

   They bought $2\frac{1}{3}$ pounds of dried fruit altogether.

2. $\frac{1}{4} + \frac{7}{12} + \frac{11}{12} = \boxed{\frac{3}{12}} + \frac{7}{12} + \frac{11}{12}$

   $= \boxed{\frac{21}{12}} = \boxed{1\frac{3}{4}}$

   She used $1\frac{3}{4}$ kilograms of flour altogether.

3. $\frac{7}{12} + \frac{3}{4} + \frac{5}{12}$

   $= \frac{7}{12} + \frac{9}{12} + \frac{5}{12} = \frac{21}{12} = \frac{7}{4} = 1\frac{3}{4}$

   The total weight of the fruit salad was $1\frac{3}{4}$ pounds.

4. $\frac{1}{3} + \frac{4}{9} = \boxed{\frac{3}{9}} + \frac{4}{9} = \boxed{\frac{7}{9}}$

   $1 - \boxed{\frac{7}{9}} = \frac{9}{9} - \boxed{\frac{7}{9}} = \boxed{\frac{2}{9}}$

   Sam spent $\frac{2}{9}$ of his time playing computer games.

5. $\frac{1}{6} + \frac{1}{3} = \boxed{\frac{1}{6}} + \boxed{\frac{2}{6}} = \boxed{\frac{3}{6}}$

   $1 - \boxed{\frac{3}{6}} = \boxed{\frac{6}{6}} - \boxed{\frac{3}{6}} = \boxed{\frac{3}{6}} = \boxed{\frac{1}{2}}$

   Latoya kept $\frac{1}{2}$ of the pizza for her grandmother.

6. $\boxed{\frac{7}{8}} + \boxed{\frac{3}{4}} = \boxed{\frac{13}{8}}$

   $\boxed{\frac{13}{8}} - \boxed{\frac{3}{8}} = \boxed{\frac{5}{4}} = \boxed{1\frac{1}{4}}$

   $1\frac{1}{4}$ liters of mixed juice was left in the jug.

7. a. $\boxed{\frac{4}{10}}$; $\boxed{\frac{4}{10}} = \boxed{\frac{2}{5}}$

   Elan gives away $\frac{2}{5}$ of his marbles.

   b. $1 - \frac{2}{5} = \frac{3}{5}$

   $\frac{3}{5}$ of the marbles are left.

8. $\frac{8}{12} = \frac{2}{3}$

   She cuts off $\frac{2}{3}$ of the ribbon.

   $1 - \frac{2}{3} = \frac{1}{3}$

   $\frac{1}{3}$ of the ribbon is left.

9. **Method 1**

$\underline{7}$ units = $\underline{\$14}$
1 unit = $\underline{\$2}$
$\underline{3}$ units = $\underline{\$2} \times \underline{3} = \underline{\$6}$
$\$14 - \$\underline{6} = \$\underline{8}$
Winton had $\$\underline{8}$ left.

Method 2

$\frac{3}{7}$ of $\$14 = \frac{3}{7} \times \$\underline{14}$

$= \frac{\$42}{7}$

$= \$\underline{6}$

He spent $\$\underline{6}$.
$\$14 - \$\underline{6} = \$\underline{8}$
Winton had $\$\underline{8}$ left.

10. **Method 1**

9 units = 621 m²
1 unit = 69 m²
5 units = 69 m² × 5 = 345 m²
621 − 345 = 276 m²
He planted tulips on 276 square meters of land.

Method 2

$\frac{5}{9}$ of 621 m² = $\frac{5}{9} \times$ 621 m²

$= \frac{3,105 \text{ m}^2}{9}$

$= 345 \text{ m}^2$

621 − 345 = 276 m²
He planted tulips on 276 square meters of land.

11. **Method 1**

3 units = 156
1 unit = 52
156 − 52 = 104
There are 104 economy-class seats.

Method 2

$\frac{1}{3}$ of 156 = $\frac{1}{3} \times$ 156

$= \frac{156}{3}$

$= 52$

156 − 52 = 104
There are 104 economy-class seats.

12. $\frac{1}{8} \times 6 = \frac{6}{8}$

$= \frac{3}{4}$

They eat $\frac{3}{4}$ of the pear altogether.

13. $\frac{2}{9} \times 12 = \frac{24}{9}$

$= 2\frac{6}{9}$

$= 2\frac{2}{3}$

Mr. Lee prepared $2\frac{2}{3}$ liters of orange juice altogether.

Worksheet 9

1.

Length of Leaves	Tally	Number of Leaves
1 cm	/	1
2 cm	/	1
3 cm	////	4
4 cm	LHT	5
5 cm	LHT /	6
6 cm	///	3
7 cm	//	2
8 cm	/	1

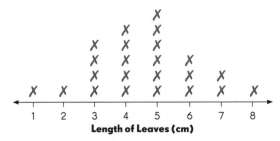

Length of Leaves (cm)

2. a. Bus
    b. Answers vary.
    c. Bicycle
    d. Answer vary.
    e. 4 − 1 = 3
       3 more children go to school by bus than by bicycle.